DEREK
FELL

F

FRANCES LINCOLN LIMITED
PUBLISHERS

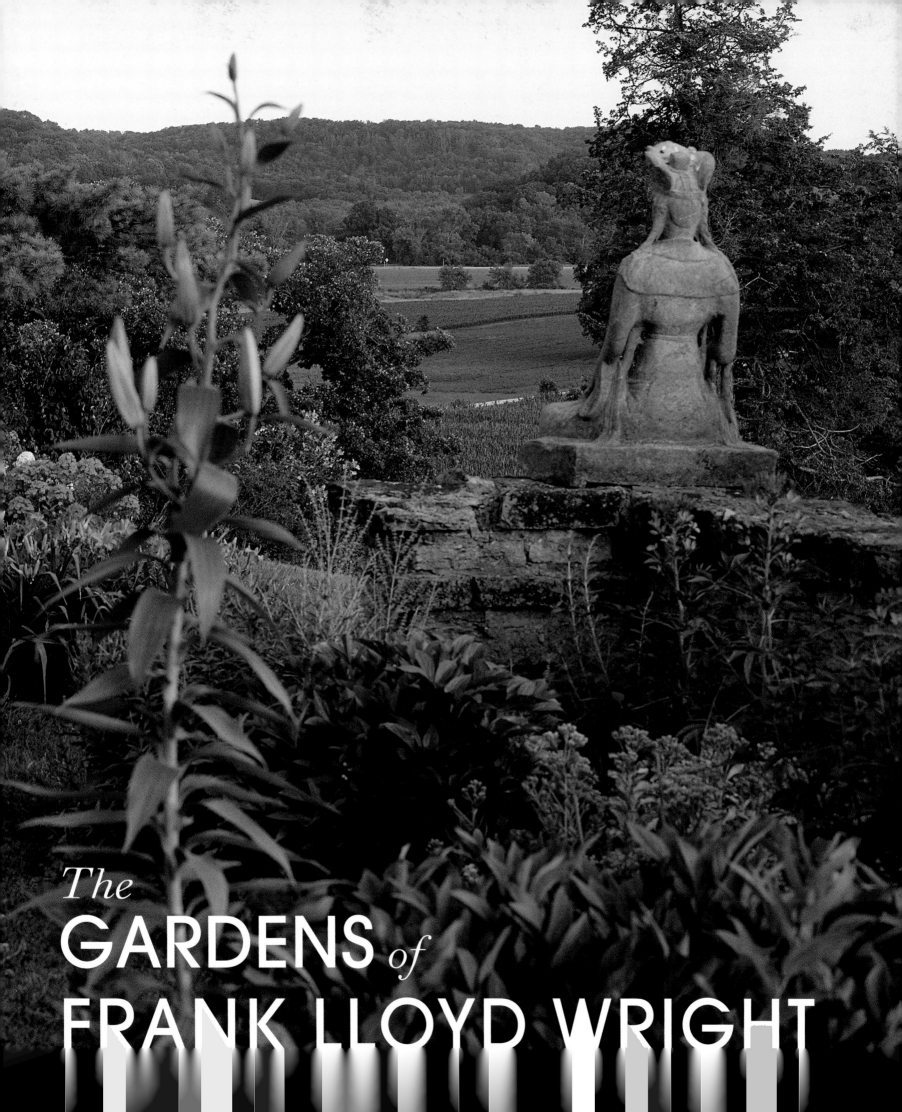

The GARDENS *of* FRANK LLOYD WRIGHT

This book is dedicated to the memory
of Frank Lloyd Wright, "The greatest
landscape architect that ever lived."

Frances Lincoln Limited
4 Torriano Mews
Torriano Avenue
London NW5 2RZ
www.franceslincoln.com

The Gardens of Frank Lloyd Wright
Copyright © 2009 Frances Lincoln Limited
Text copyright © Derek Fell

Photographs copyright © Derek Fell with the
following exceptions:
pages 10, 62 and 110 Courtesy The Frank Lloyd
Wright Foundation, Taliesin West, Scottsdale, AZ.

First Frances Lincoln edition 2009

British Library Cataloguing in Publication Data
A catalogue record for this book is available from the
British Library

ISBN: 978 0 7112 2967 9

Printed in China

9 8 7 6 5 4 3 2 1

PREVIOUS PAGE: A perennial border at Taliesin, in midsummer,
with purple coneflower, yellow daylilies, pink summer phlox and
white Kansas gayfeather in peak bloom.

RIGHT: The poker-like flowers of *Aloe vera* bloom in early spring at
Taliesin West, with the orchid tree (*Bauhinia variegata*) flowering
in the background.

OVERLEAF: Summer phlox and tiger lilies at Taliesin.

CONTENTS

A Buddha statue overlooks the plunge pool outside Wright's bedroom at Taliesin.

FOREWORD
James van Sweden

Successful designers rarely go unheralded during their lifetimes. Acknowledged as an architectural genius long before his death in 1959, Frank Lloyd Wright is no exception to this rule. However, his significant accomplishments in the realm of landscape architecture have received less attention, which is why this new, wonderfully illustrated volume by Derek Fell is so welcome.

I grew up in Grand Rapids, Michigan, and was introduced to Wright's work at an early age. On Sunday drives, my builder father would take our family to visit current job sites. We would frequently stop to admire two homes Wright designed. Although he worked on far more traditional residences, my father was fascinated by these less conventional structures. Even as a child, I realize that Wright's houses were something special.

Unlike most architects working then or now, Wright not only recognized how important the relationship between landscape and structure was to the success of his projects, he also had the ability to design within a natural setting. As these illustrations make clear, Wright was a master of architecture and landscape architecture. Confident and unafraid to obscure his architectural designs with trees or to create bold splashes of colour with plants, he created layers of beauty that resulted in a seamless exchange between inside and outside.

The elegant terraces with integrated planters that appear again and again in his residential work are perhaps the most obvious example of Wright's commitment to marrying the house to the land. But he went even further – masterfully grading the site, carefully placing the structure to take advantage of vistas, using sculpture to define space, and as Fell's research makes clear, learning the names and characteristics of plants.

It is the rare designer who works so fluidly in two mediums. Wright took advantage of everything the disciplines of architecture and landscape architecture have to offer and both professions are indebted to him. The Gardens of Frank Lloyd Wright reminds us that – ideally – our professions are intimately, even inextricably, linked.

James van Sweden is America's leading garden designer and landscape architect. He is a Fellow of the American Society of Landscape Architects and the recipient of many distinguished awards.

8

INTRODUCTION
Wright's love of nature

> *"Go to nature, thou builder of houses, consider her ways . . . Learn from Nature."*
>
> FRANK LLOYD WRIGHT

Frank Lloyd Wright (1867–1959) is world famous as an architect. He was a genius in the way he wedded stone and wood, steel and concrete, buildings and nature. Less well known – in fact, hardly known at all – is Wright's remarkable gift for landscape design and the beautiful gardens he cultivated during his lifetime, particularly at his summer home, Taliesin, and his winter home, Taliesin West.

Cornelia Brierly, landscape architect and graduate of Wright's architectural fellowship, has been associated with Wright's work for more than 75 years. When asked how she rated Wright as a landscape architect, she declared: "He was the greatest landscape architect that ever lived."

In my view, this is hardly an exaggeration. Wright's landscapes can be compared with those of the great British landscape architect, Capability Brown (1716–1783), whose work transformed the gardens of the stately homes of England; and the Brazilian, Roberto Burle Marx (1909–1994) whose acclaimed landscape projects include the promenade at Rio de Janeiro's fabulous Copacabana Beach. Like Wright, both gardened on a vast scale, altering the natural landscape to create magnificent vistas that disappear into infinity. All created lakes, bridges, woodland, hills and contours where none previously existed. Because Wright was an architect as well as a landscaper, he not only knew how best to site a residence in a particular location, and how best to improve a challenging landscape, but also where to leave nature alone, as he did at Fallingwater in Pennsylvania's rural Laurel Highlands.

Three of Wright's landscape projects are featured in a recent compilation of the world's best gardens.[1] They are Taliesin, Taliesin West, and Fallingwater, his most celebrated private commission. Taliesin presents a low, stepped profile, inspired by Tuscan villas that Wright encountered on hillsides during a stay in Italy. Taliesin West embodies Wright's desire for "organic living", the very steps, terraces, walls and courtyards linked to the harsh landscape by his use of desert stone and wood, and desert plants – such as the giant saguaro cactus – as living

---

[1] *1,001 Gardens You Must See Before You Die*, ed. Rae Spencer-Jones (Barrons/Cassell).

The upper courtyard at Taliesin with flower beds colour-coordinated to create contrasting colour harmonies – pink and blue in the central island bed, and yellow and orange in the border planting alongside Wright's work room. The entrance to Wright's living quarters is beyond the central colony of ostrich ferns.

sculptural accents. Fallingwater contrasts a modernistic design of slab-like terraces with the rugged grandeur of a waterfall and deciduous woodland, the terraces cantilevered over the falls like rock shelves. The structure offers elevated views into the treetops and there is such a dramatic view of the house and waterfall from a natural rocky observation platform downstream that it has become probably the most recognizable private residence in the world.

Wright's gardens are not only a visual delight in the form of buildings skilfully placed in the landscape, and intimate garden spaces, the ornamentation and hardscape are rich in texture and symbolism, some elements – such as sculpture – designed by himself and others by students inspired by his art. Architecture and landscape create a ying-yang dynamic, the lines of the buildings strong and masculine, the surroundings usually soft and tranquil with arching branches of trees, velvet lawns and floral beauty. The elements of each garden combine to impress – the perfect scale of everything in relation to the house, the intimacy of courtyards, the placement of water features, the design and positioning of planters, the stonework of retaining walls, balconies and shaded patios. And in the case of the two Taliesins and Fallingwater, the settings are majestic.

Taliesin occupies a hill that was once bleak prairie, and Wright manipulated everything within his view, from the garden surrounding the house to skyline plantings seen as mere silhouettes in the distance. To provide enough trees for planting the countryside he even bought out a local nursery and, with the former owner following in his footsteps, Wright stuck bamboo canes into the soil and decreed, "sumac" or "bur oak" or "willow", or some other native species, depending on the picture in his mind's eye. Head gardener Frances Nemtin recalls helping Wright to plant a 15-acre pine forest, partly as a source of fragrant evergreen boughs to decorate the interiors at Taliesin.

When I stepped into the garden at Taliesin and saw what Wright had done to create visual drama, I felt the same thrill as when I first stepped into Claude Monet's garden, at Giverny and recognized Monet's skill at creating beautiful colour harmonies. It is the landscape of an

Bougainvillea lights up the entrance to Taliesin West; beyond, water trickles from an overflowing decorative basin.

original, implemented on a scale that is staggering in its sophistication. Both Monet and Wright took inspiration from Japanese culture, but neither slavishly copied Japanese design. Each adapted it to their own aesthetic. Wright even warned against copying the designs of other cultures or other artists. "Imitation is the worst form of flattery," he insisted.

Wright was born in Richland Center, Wisconsin, 18 miles southwest of the site that was to become his second home, Taliesin. He died at his winter home, Taliesin West, at age 91. Art historian, Robert Campbell described him as "The greatest artist the US has ever produced . . ." and further declared that none of America's other great artists – its painters, sculptors and composers – ranked with Rembrandt or Michelangelo or Beethoven. "Wright alone has that standing," he concluded.

Wright's father was a Unitarian preacher and musician who moved his family from one parish to another. During Wright's childhood he lived in Rhode Island, Iowa and Massachusetts, but during his teens he spent summers in Wisconsin on his uncle James's farm, close to where he

would later build Taliesin. This farming experience taught him to see patterns and rhythms in nature that he liked to convert to abstract forms and use as inspiration for his architectural designs.

Wright's mother, Anna, was a teacher and loved beautiful buildings. She wanted him to become an architect and decorated his bedroom with scenes of cathedrals. He studied civil engineering at the University of Wisconsin but left after two years at age 20 to become an architect. He worked briefly with the Chicago architectural firm of J. Lyman Silsbee, and there availed himself of Silsbee's extensive library of books on art and architecture. At this time he began collecting Japanese woodblock prints. He then spent six years with Adler and Sullivan, a more progressive Chicago architectural firm, and was quickly promoted to chief draftsman.

The style of architecture called "Prairie School" originated with Wright's employer, the Boston-born architect Louis Sullivan, who conceived the idea of an authentic American architecture distinct from anything previously seen in Europe and suited to the needs of mid-

Westerners living in a modern age. Sullivan thought that a building should reflect the place and time in which it was built – not some long gone historic period beyond the shores of America – and be sympathetic to its site and surroundings. His designs consisted of mostly abstracted plant motifs.

Sullivan inspired a younger generation of architects to apply his organic principles to all types of buildings, and particularly residential architecture. These architects not only included Wright, but also George Grant Elmslie and William Gray Purcell (all of whom worked for Sullivan at one time or another). Between the years 1895 and 1918 they applied Sullivan's system of making the interior and exterior an integrated unit, with art-glass windows, custom furnishings and artwork specially chosen to be complementary.

The term, Prairie School was coined in 1936, chiefly to describe Sullivan's work between 1893 and 1910. It was then adopted to distinguish the work of Sullivan's followers, such as Wright. The Prairie School is now considered the most original and important contribution to American architecture.

In 1890 Wright married Catherine (Kitty) Lee Tobin with whom he had four sons and two daughters. Sullivan granted Wright a loan to enlarge his first home, at Oak Park, then a rural Chicago suburb. However, Wright left Sullivan when Sullivan realized that Wright was moonlighting – in strict violation of his employment contract. Wright set up in business for himself in 1893, at his home. He was able to add a spacious studio, and over the next sixty-six years Wright designed avant-garde houses and innovative commercial buildings, such as the earthquake-proof Imperial Hotel, Tokyo, and the Guggenheim Museum, New York. At first ridiculed for its spiral design, the Guggenheim building is now regarded as a work of art in its own right.

In 1910 Wright left Oak Park, to spend a year in Europe putting together a design portfolio with a German publisher, and also studying European art and architecture. He then returned to the area of Spring Green, Wisconsin to begin construction of Taliesin.

Wright liked to dovetail his houses into a stimulating landscape so they blend with their surroundings; this he achieved mostly by creating a low profile for the building and framing geometric architectural lines with trees or built-in terrace planters. His early work around Chicago became known as the "prairie style" as a consequence of taking inspiration from patterns found in the prairie, although he disliked this description. He hated to be pigeonholed, and felt every design he created was original.

After he settled into Taliesin, Wright planned to marry Martha Borthwick Cheney (she liked to be called Mamah – pronounced May-mah). Unfortunately, Mamah died before they could marry. When Wright's divorce from his first wife became final, he married a second time, to sculptress, Miriam Noel. This marriage soon ended in divorce and in 1928 Wright married a third time, to Olgivanna (Olga) Hinzenberg. They visited Arizona and, with her encouragement, Wright established a winter home and teaching facility in the desert, which they named Taliesin West. The school continues today as the Frank Lloyd Wright School of Architecture, with summer courses conducted at Taliesin, on a property called the Hillside Home School, originally designed as a school for two spinster aunts. Of more than 1,100 projects Wright designed during his life, one third were built after he turned 80. He won numerous awards, including the Centennial Medallion from the American Society of Landscape Architects, which declared Taliesin "A national landmark for outstanding landscape architecture."

Outside Wright's bedroom at Taliesin, tiger lilies (*Lilium lancifolium*, formerly *L. tigrinum*) decorate the courtyard, with a plunge pool overlooked by a Buddha sculpture.

This view, from the living room at Taliesin, shows gardening on a grand scale. Here, Wright dammed a stream to create a pair of lakes, and planted white pines and bur oaks.

17

In his site plans Wright often showed meticulous border plantings or made notes about framing the property with trees. For example, the plan for the Christian House, West Lafayette, Indiana, shows precise locations for trees and a notation stating: "Near the building use low species of evergreen (horizontal junipers, pfitzer junipers, mugo pine). On north boundary of property use high species of evergreen (American arborvitae, white pine, Scotch pine, red pine, Norway spruce, blue spruce and Chinese arborvitae). Use above high growing species also on the south west blocks of property where indicated on drawing. Plant these about 4 to 5 ft on center in groups of three, four and five."

For his Little House, Peoria, Illinois, a specific planting plan for a long border shows flowering shrubs (such as Persian lilac, hardy shrub hibiscus and mock-orange) and perennials by botanical name. For a massed planting of perennial summer phlox he even specifies variety names: 'Independence', 'Lady Napier', 'Boule de Feu and 'Miss Lingard', in company with prairie wildflowers, such as liatris, helenium and boltonia.

Wright's son, Lloyd joined his father in business at age 19, travelling to Italy to help on Wright's monograph, and afterwards he toured European gardens. Landscape architecture soon became his passion, and back in the USA, he joined the leading landscape firm of Olmsted and Olmsted. Lloyd later worked on many of his father's projects, notably on the landscaping for Wright's California houses.

Wright, however, did not alter nature for the sake of it. When asked by the owners of Fallingwater for landscaping ideas, Wright considered the building so skilfully integrated with its surroundings, he advised them not to change the natural landscape since it could not be improved upon.

The Great Depression of 1930 and the years leading up to World War II were lean years for Wright, and he devised several ways to avoid bankruptcy – one by selling shares in himself to affluent friends in the belief that times would change (indeed they did), and by charging students for a year's tuition to study with him. He also offered more-affordable, moderately priced homes that he called Usonian, characterized by large, comfortable living spaces around a dominant central fireplace, and small kitchens, bedrooms

and bathrooms. Views from the living area generally faced a secluded side, with views of a meadow, woodland or coastline.

Publicity surrounding Wright's Fallingwater, which was completed in 1937, renewed interest in his work, and from that time until his death he never lacked commissions. He always designed with an intense personal attachment to his homes, even to the point of rearranging furniture or requesting that the curtains be changed when he revisited his clients in their houses.

Never content to be merely an architect, Wright was keenly interested in the broader aspects of artistic expression and social issues. He was a pacifist, and during World War II encouraged his apprentices to become conscientious objectors. His popularity among architectural students reached a cult status, particularly after his third marriage.

Until his death in 1959 Wright continued to change Taliesin and Taliesin West. Taliesin was his main residence and the longest ongoing architectural and landscaping project of his career. It is regarded as the most complete embodiment of what Wright thought, how he lived, and how he landscaped.

LEFT: The entrance to Wright's Oak Park studio with the living quarters at the rear. Wright designed the dish-shaped pedestal planters and worked with sculptor Richard Bock on the design of the figures behind them. Entitled *The Boulders*, the sculptures show men attempting to free themselves from bondage.

OVERLEAF: Fallingwater, Wright's most famous private commission, with its dramatic series of cantilevered terraces jutting out over a roaring cascade, framed by autumn leaves.

OAK PARK
and early influences (1889–1909)

Wright occupied his first home and studio, at Oak Park, a Chicago suburb, from 1889 until 1909. There he raised six children with his first wife, Kitty. Wright's mother, Anna also lived on the property, in a cottage that predates Wright's home. The site is a wooded corner lot at Chicago Avenue and Forest Avenue that had previously served as a plant nursery owned by a Scots nurseryman and landscaper. At the time it was surrounded by open prairie. An ancient ginkgo tree from the original nursery stills shades part of the building, and when Wright built a passageway between his studio and living quarters, he built around a locust tree rather than sacrifice it to his plan.

Wright was twenty-one and his wife eighteen when they married. Since then, the area has become an affluent residential district, and during its urbanization he obtained numerous commissions to build houses in the neighbourhood so that today it's possible to view fourteen of his designs within easy walking distance.

The steeply pitched roofs of the Oak Park house and studio create a triangle similar to the tee-pee shape of shelters made by plains Indians, but later additions to the main residence feature flat, elongated roof lines that achieve a unified design more typical of his early "prairie style". In Wright's day, his children stabled ponies in a barn on the property, and Wright stabled his own horse across Forest Avenue, later parking a saucy yellow Stoddard Dayton roadster at the curb. Along the driveway were pens for chickens and pigeons. These bird shelters have since been removed and the stables converted to a bookstore.

Although the original garden space has been severely reduced, especially after Wright built his studio, significant features remain. In particular is an apron of lawn facing the entrance to the house, many mature shade trees and several

OPPOSITE: The entrance to Wright's Oak Park home, showing a steeply pitched roof reminiscent of the triangular-shaped tee-pees used by Native Americans of the Plains whose culture he admired.

LEFT: At the side entrance to the Oak Park studio a *Sprite* statue faces a small courtyard shaded by a ginkgo tree.

A semi-circular brick patio is shaded by the graceful branches of a serviceberry tree (*Amelanchier canadensis*). The patio was a favourite place for Wright to read and wind down after work.

significant hardscape features, such as a spacious semicircular brick patio where Wright liked to read in a rocking chair. Shaded by trees, it faces the lawn that leads to a screening hedge, of forsythia, at the edge of the sidewalk.

The studio entry porch is rich in ornamental detail. A pair of brick columns crowned with dish planters overflows with plants, and these planters serve as sentinels to a porch roof that is supported by square columns featuring carved storks by sculptor Richard Bock. Flanking the stork sculptures is a pair of chunky stone sculptures of men wrestling to be freed from the earth, symbolic of Wright's quest to throw off artistic convention. Wright designed the

planters, using his logo of a square surrounding a circle as the basis for the shallow dish design.

The house incorporates many features that Wright would use time and again to connect with nature. For example, the brick porch sentinels and their verdant planters are clearly visible from the house and studio interior through windows. Three glass skylights he designed feature abstract patterns of tree foliage, adding comforting green accents to rooms, like a tree canopy. Many of the rooms – though spacious and with high, domed ceilings – drop down low at the edges to bring views of the garden into focus. Wright called this aspect of design "compression and release" so

the experience of walking into a spacious, high-ceilinged space is heightened by the low entry. Wright also created the sensation of compression and release outdoors, in his later landscapes, using low, shady pergolas to compress a walkway leading to a sunlit open space, or by using a tunnel of leaves for a similar sensation.

Wright designed much of the furniture for his home and those of his clients, though he admitted that he often sacrificed comfort for beauty. Tall vases filled with dried wayside wildflowers and weeds feature in most of the rooms, linking the interior with nature, while space on windowsills is provided for potted plants to soften the

home's architectural geometry. Wright referred to his arrangements of wayside plants as "weedscapes", and cherished a collection of palms for indoor decoration.

Wright so loved dried flower arrangements for his houses that he designed special vases to display them in. He also took inspiration for glass and window patterns from dried weeds, creating designs from shapes of leaves or seed heads. Windows in the Robie House, Chicago (see page 127) feature abstract patterns of wheat stalks, while wayside plant shapes, autumn colours and prairie grasses are represented in the more than four hundred glass panels designed by Wright for the Dana House, Springfield, Illinois.

The pillars at the entrance to Oak Park are decorated with carvings designed in cooperation with sculptor Richard Bock. They show storks – wise birds – with the book of learning beneath the tree of knowledge.

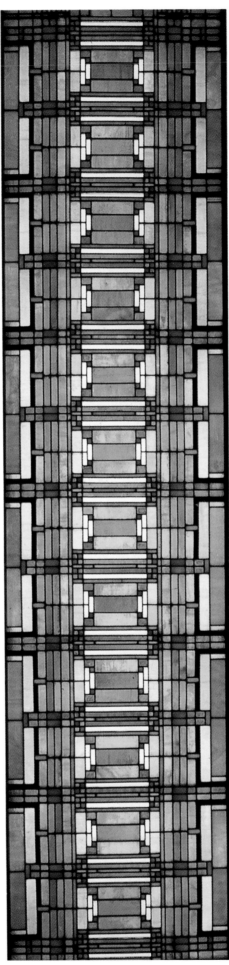

The foliage of a walnut tree (*Juglans nigra*) at Taliesin backlit by the sun shows the probable inspiration for a pair of coloured glass skylights, representing an abstraction of tree foliage, that Wright designed for the reception hall of his house.

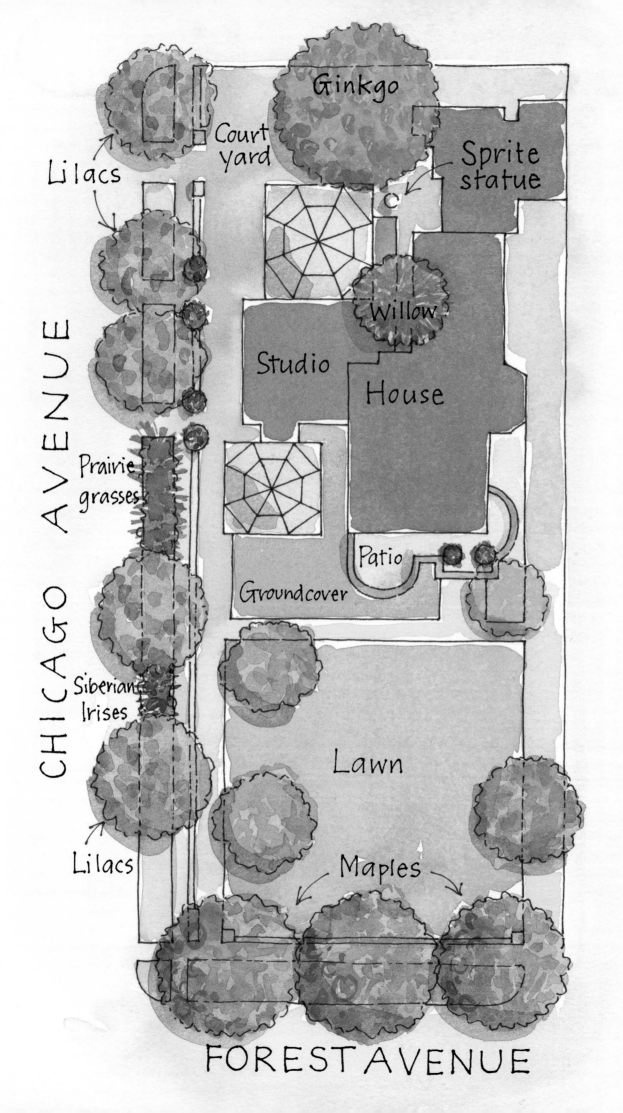

OPPOSITE: An outline plan
of Wright's Oak Park home
and studio.

BELOW: Dried flower heads of
wild dock – a wayside weed –
beside a field of mature oats
at Taliesin. It was from such
encounters with nature that
Wright drew inspiration for his
designs. Brown and beige are
the restful combination he
called "earth tones".

After leaf drop in fall, many trees and shrubs offer beautiful branch silhouettes to mix with wayside weeds, particularly corkscrew willow and burning bush with its herringbone branch pattern. Wright looked for such patterns everywhere in nature, and mixed bare branches with interesting shapes among his dried flowers and grasses. A mass planting of switch grass (*Panicum virgatum*) greets visitors to the studio entrance of Oak Park.

The interior colours at Oak Park are what Wright called "earth tones", particularly beige and brown which Wright considered the most soothing colour combination in nature. Beige is the colour of prairie grass in autumn and brown the colour of oak leaves and dried dock seed heads in autumn.

During Wright's occupancy of the Oak Park property, the European Arts and Crafts movement was a popular topic for discussion among Chicago artists, and Wright joined a local Arts and Crafts club to promote its principles. Arts and Crafts was an aesthetic movement that evolved in Europe during the latter half of the nineteenth century. The leading proponent was William Morris whose designs for beautiful furniture, wallpapers, tapestries, curtains, carpets and even books rebelled against both the ostentation of the Victorian era and the soullessness of industrialization in favour of simplicity and the use of natural materials and hand-crafted construction. Morris summed up his credo by the following statement: "If I were asked what is at once the most beautiful production of Art . . . I should answer, A Beautiful House; and . . . the next to be longed for . . . a Beautiful Book. To enjoy good houses and good books in self respect and decent comfort seems to me to be the most pleasurable end towards which all human beings ought now to struggle."

In addition to the work of William Morris, Wright admired the work of the Glasgow architect Charles Rennie Mackintosh who was also noted for his glasswork and furniture designs, so that for him, as for Wright, the exterior and interior of his buildings became a homogenous whole. Mackintosh made beautiful watercolour paintings of flowers and used these studies to create abstract patterns, especially for windows and skylights, as did Wright.

Speaking of the Arts and Crafts movement, Wright

wrote: "Good William Morris and John Ruskin were much in evidence in Chicago intellectual circles . . . The Mackintoshes of Scotland, restless European protestants [innovators] also – Van de Velde of Belgium, Berlage of Holland, Adolphe Loos and Otto Wagner of Vienna; all were genuine protestants [innovators], but then seen and heard only in Europe." Of the great British Arts and Crafts architect, Edwin Lutyens, he declared: "To appraise the work of this great Englishman I am incompetent." Wright's narrow, vertical corner windows for Fallingwater and other buildings emulate windows Lutyens designed. Nevertheless Wright faulted him for too much similarity in his residential designs and a failure to change with the times.

Wright's Oak Park studio attracted a number of talented architectural students, and the facility became a hive of experimentation and innovation. Students in particular liked to imitate Wright's distinctive style of dress, including long hair, floppy ties, high starched collars and the habit of working in a smock. Under Wright's direction the students worked as a close-knit team, and during this Oak Park period Wright completed 125 commissions.

Perhaps the best example of Wright's "prairie style" residence during this period is the Robie House, in Chicago. Built in 1909, it is today owned by the University of Chicago and open to the public (see page 127). Shoehorned into a very narrow lot that leaves little room for foundation plantings or garden, it shows elements of both Japanese and Mayan influences in its architecture, although Wright did not like the word "inspiration" applied to any of his work. When a friend sent him a draft of a tribute to his work, Wright objected to a reference to Japanese influences, and suggested it would be more accurate to say that he "digested" Japanese architecture. Even so, Japanese elements show in the way the Robie House room interiors are spacious and low, each room flowing into the next, and Mayan in the way that Wright incorporated long planters the length and width of the building, so even though there is no room for a front garden, plants can drape down and create curtains of outdoor foliage similar to the way Mayan architecture supports terraces of plants after centuries of abandonment and encroachment by the jungle.

The Mayan influence

In 1839, New York-based John L. Stephens, a travel writer, and Frederick Catherwood, an illustrator, astonished the world when they returned from an expedition into the Yucatan Peninsula with the first images of Mayan lost cities: notably Chichan Itza, Tulum, Copan, Quirigua, Palenque, and Uxmal. Their book, *Incidents of Travel in Central America, Chiapas and Yucatan* not only describes their intrepid adventures into almost impenetrable jungle, but it also contains Catherwood's fantastic illustrations showing immense buildings buried under vegetation for centuries. The following year they returned to the Yucatan for seven months of further exploration. This resulted in the publication of a second book, *Incidents of Travel in Yucatan* (1843).

Catherwood's illustrations are amazing, for they have an almost supernatural quality. Every image presents an aura of isolation, solid stone structures completely surrounded by jungle that had overwhelmed the sites for centuries after the cities were mysteriously abandoned. The buildings include pyramids, nunneries, palaces, places of worship and observatories. Even after the expedition cleared the sites, level areas remained adorned with tropical creepers. Flat roofs and terraces sprouted vegetation so the buildings appear to be outgrowths of the lush terrain. Mist swirls onto the tops of palm trees, and Catherwood shows incredible details of stonework and ornamentation.

'The designs were strange and incomprehensible," wrote Stephens. "Very elaborate, sometimes grotesque, but often simple, tasteful and beautiful. Among the intelligible subjects are squares and diamonds, with busts of human beings, heads of leopards, and compositions of leaves and flowers, and the ornaments known everywhere as *greques*. The ornaments, which succeed each other, are all different; the whole form an extraordinary mass of richness and complexity, and the effect is both grand and curious . . . Each stone, by itself, was an unmeaning fractional part; but placed by the side of the others, helped make a whole, without which it would be incomplete."

The images pleased Wright. In his book, *A Testament* (1957), Wright explained their influence on his work:

The Mayan ruins at Tulum, Yucatan, by Frederick Catherwood (*top*), one of the illustrations that so inspired Wright. The entrance to Wright's living quarters at Taliesin West (*below*) shows the Mayan influence.

"Mighty, primitive abstractions of man's nature – ancient arts of the Mayan, the Inca, the Tolcec. These great American abstractions were all earth-architectures: gigantic masses of masonry raised up on great stone-paved terrain, all planned as one mountain, one vast plateau lying there or made into the real mountain ranges themselves; these vast areas of paved earth walled by stone construction. These were human creations, cosmic as sun, moon and stars! . . . a grandeur arose in the scale of total building never since excelled, seldom equalled." Early in his career, in 1905, Wright expressed a desire to see Mayan and Inca ruins for himself. "I wished I might someday have enough money to go to Mexico, Guatamala and Peru to join in excavating those long slumbering remains of lost cultures; mighty primitive abstractions of man's nature." It is not known if Wright ever did see those archeological ruins. His eldest son, Lloyd claims he went to Mexico's Yucatan during the 1910s to study Mayan architecture, but there is no record

A Japanese screen used in Wright's living quarters at Taliesin West. The vertical divisions of the folding screen inspired Wright's liking for windows without curtains, so that their frames made exterior views resemble the partitions of a Japanese screen.

of the trip. He certainly saw life-size plaster cast replicas of Mayan buildings at the World's Columbian Exposition (the World's Fair), Chicago, in 1893.

The Mayan look is especially evident in a series of buildings Wright designed in the vicinity of Los Angeles, California, notably in the Hollyhock House, a residence he designed for oil heiress Aline Barnsdall and in La Miniatura, a house for a wealthy widow, Alice Millard, in Pasadena. For these buildings Wright designed special "textured blocks", interlocking pre-cast concrete squares patterned with Mayan-like design motifs to create a unique architectural design that blended two cultures – Mayan and Western. Perhaps even more startling was Wright's blending of Mayan and Japanese cultures in his design for the interiors of Tokyo's Imperial Hotel, and also in the exterior of Wright's Yamamura House – an abstracted

Mayan temple – built for the president of a Japanese sake brewery, in 1924.

Wright's liking for the blending of cultures is obvious from murals used to decorate rooms of his Oak Park property. In two separate wall decorations Wright shows a plains Indian dressed in Egyptian clothes, making the Indian look particularly regal.

The Japanese influence

Wright's first visit to Japan occurred in 1905 when he travelled by steamship from San Francisco to Tokyo with his wife and former clients, Mr and Mrs. Ward W. Willits. He took photographs of all that impressed him, the majority showing details of gardens and landscapes. In particular Wright admired the way Japanese buildings, gardens and landscapes seemed to blend seamlessly into each other.

"The cultivated fields rising tier upon tier to still higher terraced vegetable fields, green-dotted. And extending far above the topmost dotted fields, (we) see the mountain tops themselves . . . For pleasure in all this human affair you couldn't tell where the architecture leaves off and the garden begins."

Japanese influence had already made its impact upon European art, particularly in the work of the great French Impressionist painters. Cézanne, Monet, Renoir and Van Gogh all admired Japanese art, notably the work of Hiroshige and his woodblock prints. Like the early Impressionists, Wright was captivated by the animated style of Japanese artists, including the way that their screens show a panoramic view of the countryside or a detail of nature – such as a sweep of water irises or a field of poppies – in five-piece segments, as though looking through a wide window divided by vertical lines. Wright wrote: "Ever since I discovered the Japanese print, Japan has appealed to me as the most romantic, the most artistic country on earth and a more ingenious product of native conditions of life and work, therefore more nearly 'modern' as I saw it, than any European civilization alive or dead."

Japanese buildings at the 1893 World's Columbian Exposition in Chicago, as well as many published sources, inspired Wright's work. His first trip to Japan lasted six months; his second trip, in 1913, was to secure the commission for the Imperial Hotel, in Tokyo. "Japanese buildings, like rocks and trees, grew in their places. Their gardens were idealized pattern of their landscapes," he noted. In particular he marvelled at the scenery surrounding Yokohama Bay: "Imagine, if you can, sloping foothills and mountainsides, all 'antique' sculpture, carved century after century, with curving terraces. The cultivated fields, green dotted. And extending far above the topmost dotted fields are seen the very mountaintops themselves corrugated with regular rows of young pine trees pushing diagonally over . . . pattern everywhere visible." The Imperial Hotel opened in 1922 to worldwide praise. Resembling an Imperial Japanese palace, it had a wide, low profile. But the interiors are distinctly Mayan in appearance, using massive pitted stone blocks to simulate weathered Mayan stonework. Its unique

foundation design helped the hotel to survive a severe earthquake the following year that levelled most of Tokyo. However, owing to rising property values and the need to add considerably more rooms, the hotel was demolished in 1968 and replaced with a larger, more mundane structure. Fortunately, out of respect for Wright's work, the entrance lobby and pool were rebuilt at the Meija-Mura museum.

When Wright concluded the building of the Imperial Hotel he wrote about his achievement: "The Imperial Hotel is designed as a system of gardens and sunken gardens and terraced gardens – of balconies that are gardens and loggias that are also gardens – and roofs that are gardens – until the whole arrangement becomes an interpretation of gardens. Japan is garden-land ."

By 1909 Wright's architecture had become well known and greatly admired, but his domestic life suffered, complicated by his affair with Mamah Cheney. An opportunity to work with her and a German publisher on a portfolio of his designs allowed him to escape the scandal surrounding the affair. After a year he returned, but he and his wife were unable to reconcile, and so he decided to create a new home for himself and Mrs. Cheney close to his Wisconsin roots at Spring Green. He called the new home

The Nathan G. Moore House at Oak Park, showing Wright's use of a decorative balustrade to separate the garden from the sidewalk. The house displays a combination of architectural styles – Tudor for the roof and Gothic for the ground floor.

Containers filled with sweet potato vines (*Ipomoea batatas*) decorate the entrance to the Edward R. Hills House at Oak Park, displaying Wright's characteristic use of planters – rather than foundation plantings – to embellish the structure and soften bold architectural lines.

Taliesin – pronounced Tal-ee-ay-sin (see pages 38–63).

By 1925 Wright's children were grown and his wife moved from Oak Park to downtown Chicago. The Oak Park property was sold and later subdivided into rental units. Several years before his death in 1959 Wright returned in order to restore the buildings to their appearance in 1909, the last year of his residency. The subsequent restoration took thirteen years to complete. In 1974 the Frank Lloyd Wright Home and Studio Foundation was formed to work with the National Trust for Historic Preservation to preserve the property and open it for tours.

Wright designs around Oak Park

Just minutes from Wright's Oak Park home and studio are twenty-five Wright buildings, mostly private residences, but visible from the street. Of particular interest are the Arthur Heurtley house, the Nathan Moore house and the Edward R. Hill house, all located on Forest Avenue.

The Arthur Heurtley house emphasizes Wright's liking for a horizontal style. Of brick construction and featuring a large central chimney and low pitched roof, it has an unusual entrance in the form a v-shaped wall that partly hides a high arched entrance doorway framed by trees; the wall is decorated by planters.

Across the street is the Moore house, notable for the way Wright combined two ancient architectural styles – Tudor and Gothic – to create an imposing modern residence. Although at one time there was a sunken garden and a substantial pergola that connected it with an adjacent house occupied by Moore's daughter and son-in-law – the Edward R. Hill house – Wright's original garden design was changed after a fire caused considerable damage to the structures and shade trees. Still in place are several prominent stone balustrades and a low boundary wall with a semi-circular curvature to accommodate a mature tree Wright wanted to save, but which has since died.

The Hill house is a contrast of white stucco and black trim, softened by a pair of planters that stand as sentinels to the front porch, and a window-box planter that runs the length of three windows facing the street.

The entrance to the Arthur B. Heurtley House, Oak Park, showing Wright's preference for relatively sparse foundation plantings in favour of window box and pedestal planters.

The rounded forms and bright colours of plants spilling over their beds softens the linear geometry of these stone steps; they lead from Wright's upper courtyard at Taliesin to a stone meeting circle and guest apartments.

2 TALIESIN, Wright's summer home (1911)

The three-thousand-acre estate of Frank Lloyd Wright is called Taliesin; this was the name of a Welsh poet, and it means "shining brow" in the Welsh language. The name is an acknowledgement of Wright's roots and also the artful way that the building fits unobtrusively into the prairie hillside, as though it is an outgrowth of stratified rock. His forebears were farmers who had emigrated from Wales to the area of Spring Green, Wisconsin. At a bend in the wide Wisconsin River they farmed the prairie. Here, its sandbars give the impression of an inlet of an ocean, and its green hills dotted with indigenous oaks resemble the slopes of Snowdonia and its Welsh oaks. Winters are cold and generally there is snow cover during January and February. Spring is cool and bright green from the fresh young leaves of deciduous trees; Autumn is also cool, and a blaze of russet colours. Summers are sunny, and days are often hot. Sweet corn, watermelons and tomatoes ripen quickly outdoors during summer, and the waysides are a sea of colour from prairie wildflowers such as purple coneflower, yellow black-eyed Susans and pink monarda.

Wright designed the house, furnishings, approach roads and gardens. He also created the spectacular vistas that extend miles into the surrounding landscape of hills, meadows, cultivated fields and woodland. Even though the property was reduced to six hundred acres after Wright's death in order to settle debts and death duties, as far as the eye can see the land is farmed according to principles established by Wright. He manipulated the land not only to make the property productive and largely self-sufficient, but also to provide pleasing contours and shadow patterns that change according to the time of day and the season. You cannot speak of the "garden" at Taliesin without including everything within view, for Wright was as ruthless in manipulating all within his sight to his aesthetic ideal as Capability Brown. The famous English landscape architect

" The Valley will bloom in your hands. "

FRANK LLOYD WRIGHT'S MOTHER, ANNA

sought a pastoral Eden and spearheaded the movement away from French formality towards a more natural appearance, using meadows cropped by sheep, man-made lakes, dells and ha-has (sunken walls that do not interfere with a view), to create a harmonious arrangement of contrasting textures, colours and atmospheric effects. Similarly with Wright; he uprooted trees he disliked and replaced them with others he wanted as dominant features in the landscape, particularly oaks, birch and pine. "A tree out of place is a weed," he declared when a client objected to Wright's instruction to cut down a mature oak. He made a beautiful lake where none previously existed by damming a small stream, and he introduced livestock into the landscape for decorative effect.

Judging from a description in his *Autobiography*, Wright considered Taliesin more of a garden than a home. "Yes, Taliesin should be a garden," he wrote. "And a farm behind a workshop and a home. I saw it all, and planted it all, and laid the foundation of herd, flocks, stable, and fowls as I laid the foundation of the house. It was to be a complete living unit genuine in point of comfort and beauty, yes from pig to proprietor."

Wright would have been delighted with art critic Robert Campbell's summary of Taliesin, writing in the *Architectural Record*: "Taliesin is not so much a built object as an architectural garden that Wright seeded and weeded for almost half a century." He concluded: "There is no greater work of American art ."

The graceful contours of the bean field below Taliesin are part of the landscape Wright manipulated to make the views surrounding his home a blend of pastoral and natural spaces.

Wright bought the Log Cabin Tavern and a service station to demolish them for he considered these "nuisance buildings" – eyesores. He also bought up farmhouses and demolished the buildings to make the landscape look more rural. He considered most structures of the Midwest only temporary, unlike the great mansions he admired in Europe and on Southern plantations. He burned to the ground the tavern and a nearby farmhouse simultaneously, and negotiated with the Wisconsin Power and Light Company to relocate power lines that entered his valley. Before he was satisfied with the views at Taliesin Wright eliminated thirty-two "nuisance buildings" from his view.

Wright advocated contour ploughing, as Thomas Jefferson had, in order to prevent soil erosion. Contour ploughing, which follows the natural curvature of the landscape, also allowed Wright to play with colours, for example contrasting great sweeps of golden grain like a meandering stream between ribbons of green corn and soy beans. Students from the University of Wisconsin department of agriculture even visited Wright's Taliesin to study his contoured fields.

A series of linked flagstone courtyards surround the house, and provide seclusion, while stone terraces allow views out into the countryside in all directions. The courtyards create

a transition from Wright's interiors; these employ low ceilings and wide windows to provide spectacular views into the garden and beyond into the pristine valley. The scale of the landscaping is so vast, it seems like a super human accomplishment. Every tree, every mirror of water, every flight of steps, the orchards, vineyards, agricultural fields and hedgerows are so precisely placed that all the way to the horizon the hand of a master landscaper is evident.

He decreed that lines between rough and cultivated plantings should be clearly defined as part of the overall composition, thus emphasizing a working garden as distinct from one less obviously groomed. "Yes, there must be a natural house, not natural as caves and log cabins, but native in spirit and making," he wrote. House and landscape had to blend. The elevation above the valley excited him – the modelling of the hills, the weaving and the fabric of the woods that clung to them – the look of it tender green in spring and often tinted with snow in winter. He admired the dark greens of summer and made plantings to produce blazing colours in autumn. "I was part of it," he said, referring to the landscape.

The house plus a studio annex, staff quarters, and a guest house were laid out in a rectangle, angled to allow panoramic views of the entire valley, even to the wide Wisconsin River, with the south-east side open to the sun. The space inside the buildings, Wright designed as a series of interconnecting courtyards sunk below the crest of the hill for added shelter and privacy. At the peak of the hill he placed a broad grassy lawn edged with wide perennial borders, the rich soil held level with the lawn by means of stone retaining walls. These offer elevated views of the valley as though one is on a grassy cliff-top.

Today, the Taliesin Valley has more woodland on its hillsides than in Wright's day because of a decline in grazing. For Wright, cattle grazing in the valley added a living harmony, and their importance to him as a landscape feature is revealed in a conversation he had with his dairyman, Jack Sangster. Wright complained to him that his Guernsey cows were not producing enough cream, and so Sangster recommended they switch to Holsteins. Wright thought over the proposal for a moment and replied:

LEFT: A stone planter below the main house, with a view of the lakes beyond. Built as part of a retaining wall that sheltered cold frames for starting vegetable transplants, the planter features maiden grass (*Miscanthus sinensis*) and summer annuals.

BELOW: The upper courtyard at Taliesin and the island bed with pink phlox, red beebalm (*Monarda*) and blue salvia.

"Jack, Holsteins are black and white. Black and white on green? No; black and white do not look good on green. Never bring anything black and white or red and white in the way of an animal in sight of my eyes – coffee and cream, which are the colour of my Guernseys, on green, are the three most restful colours you can find. That is why I have Guernseys, and why I want nothing but Guernseys ."

In his autobiography, Wright revealed another reason why he admired cows in the landscape: "Why is any cow . . . always in just the right place for a picture in any landscape? Like the cypress trees of Italy, she is never wrongly placed. Her outlines quiet down so well whatever contours surround her. A group in a landscape is an enchantment."

In an essay entitled *The Japanese Print*, Wright credited the Japanese silkscreen print for much of his inspiration in architectural design, and also in garden design. "Ever since I discovered the Japanese print Japan has appealed to me as the most romantic artistic country on earth and a more indigenous product of native conditions of life and work; therefore more nearly 'modern' as I saw it, than any European civilization alive or dead."

With specific reference to garden design, Wright wrote of the Japanese aesthetic: "Pass now through building after building, separate buildings joined together with narrow open-sided corridors . . . Glimpse little courts as you go, filled with strange plants and flowers in graceful pots. Little cages of fireflies hang to the posts, as post by post we pass along the open corridors against the outside dark. Finally, all will open along one entire room-side to an enchanted scene: The Japanese Garden!"

The Oriental-style courtyards at Taliesin are positioned in series within the building. They are on different levels, adjoining the living quarters. Cupped within the walls of the main residence and studio annex, these are not imitations of Japanese gardens, with their bonsai'd tree shapes, stone lanterns and raked gravel, but the result of a fusion of Western and Asian ideas. The intimate courtyards flow into each other, with beautiful Japanese and Chinese artefacts strategically placed to introduce an Asian flavour.

One of Wright's apprentices, Edgar Tafel, in an article entitled *Apprentice to Genius*, expressed the courtyard

A mixed perennial border at Taliesin, with a statue of a Chinese deity atop the retaining wall. Perennial sunflower (*Heliopsis helianthodes*) and yarrow (*Achillea*) bloom in the foreground.

An outline plan
of Taliesin.

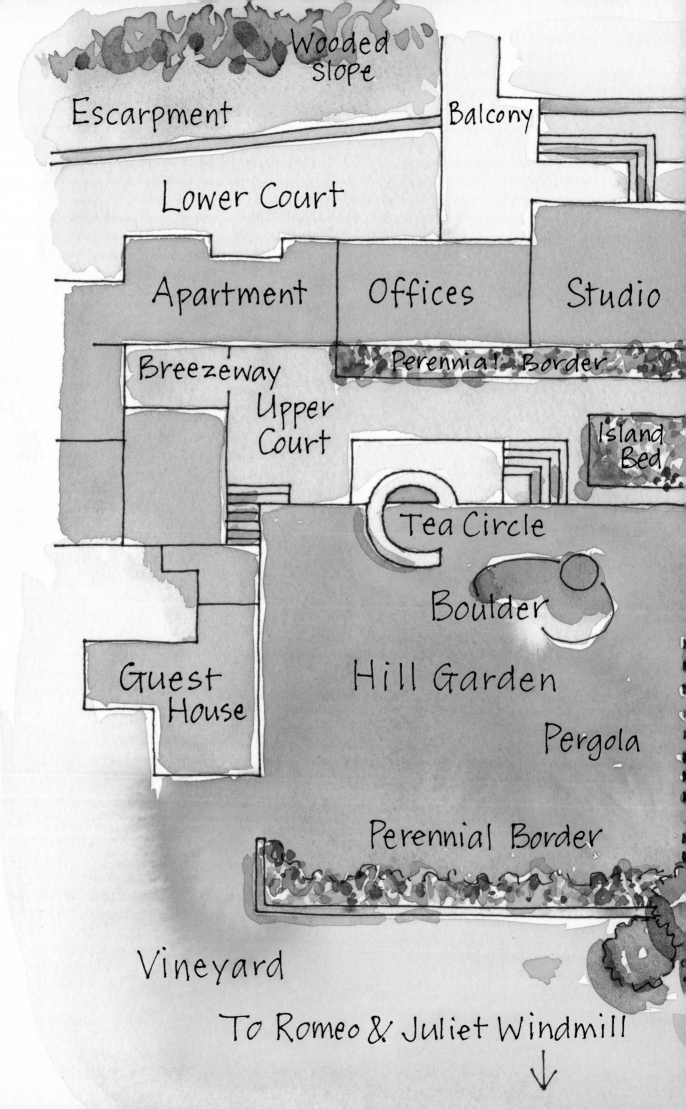

Wooded slope

Escarpment

Balcony

Lower Court

Apartment   Offices   Studio

Breezeway   Perennial Border

Upper
Court   Island
Bed

Tea Circle

Boulder

Guest   Hill Garden
House
Pergola

Perennial Border

Vineyard

To Romeo & Juliet Windmill

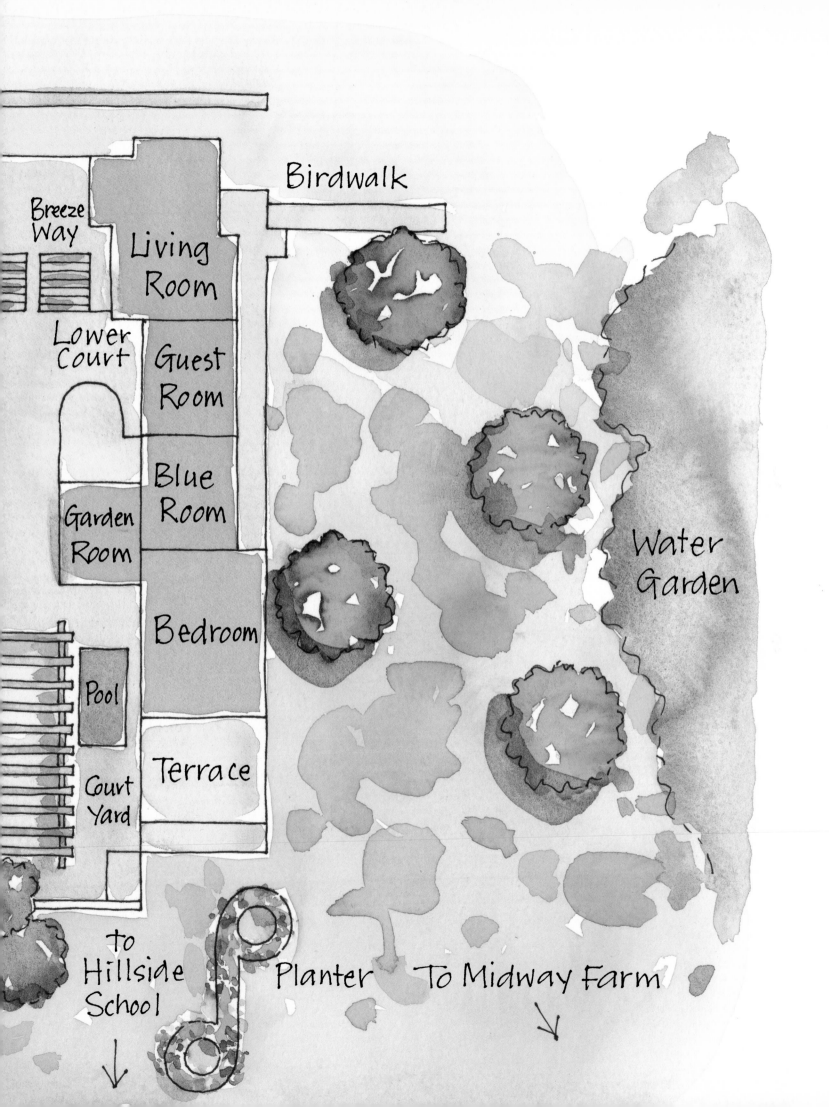

Breeze Way

Living Room

Lower Court

Guest Room

Blue Room

Garden Room

Bedroom

Pool

Terrace

Court Yard

Birdwalk

Water Garden

To Hillside School

Planter

To Midway Farm

49

RIGHT: An overall view of the upper courtyard at Taliesin showing summer plantings, with Wright's living quarters in the background.

BELOW: The upper courtyard at Taliesin seen from Wright's bedroom, with the flower-filled central island bed and, beyond the perennial border, Wright's work room on the right.

design philosophy as follows: "However much of a 'shining brow' the house might appear from the valley, it is the quality of privacy expressed behind it by the courtyards which finally count the most – historically, psychologically, and geographically. These four elevated enclosures make possible the miracle of being there in Wisconsin and at the same time somewhere in the Orient."

So much did Wright admire Japanese artisans that he spent his entire fee of $300,000 for designing Tokyo's Imperial Hotel on Japanese and Chinese artefacts. They arrived at Taliesin through Spring Green by the trainload (although much of this was destroyed by fire in 1924). Among the shipments was a wild rose from Japan that Wright planted at Taliesin, but it too perished. "Wright loved wild roses," head gardener Frances Nemtin, recalls.

The courtyards themselves are introspective, each drawing the eye inwards to a structural accent such as a fountain or a sculpture, in the Japanese style known as a cup garden, which itself evolved from Chinese garden design. Beyond these comforting enclosed spaces is the wider and dynamic landscape of Taliesin – the vistas that extend out from the terraces and balconies surrounding the residence, and also from a multitude of windows along the house interior bedrooms and living rooms. Each window is specifically designed to show a part of the valley, framed as though it is a wall painting or a Japanese folding screen. None of the windows have curtains or drapes, the better to take in panoramic views.

'Landscape seen through the openings of the building thus placed and proportioned, has greater charm than when seen independent of the architecture," Wright wrote. "Architecture properly studied in relation to the natural features surrounding it, is a greater clarifier and developer of the beauty of the landscape," he concluded.

This framing effect Wright continued outdoors, for he would make "windows" with canopies and gaps in foliage. He even placed pines with pencil straight trunks to break up the wide panorama into windows, the lower branches pruned away for clear views through the trunks.

LEFT: Tiger lilies in bloom under the pergola at Taliesin which leads uphill to the upper courtyard. Wright liked pergolas for the sensation of compression, under the pergola, and release when one stepped out into the sunlight.

OVERLEAF: The windows of Wright's living room at Taliesin look over the lakes to the wooded hills beyond. Like the divisions of a Japanese painted screen, the unadorned windows provide a panoramic view and also provide individual frames for landscape features that Wright manipulated all the way to the horizon.

51

"This modest human program arranged itself around the hilltop in a series of four varied courts, together forming a sort of drive along the hillside flanked by low buildings on one side and the flower garden on the other," he wrote of his connecting Taliesin courtyards.

An unusual landscape structure at Taliesin is the bird walk, a narrow open balcony that extends out into the tops of nearby trees from Wright's living room. It allows a spectacular bird's-eye view of the valley and also proximity to songbirds that roost in the topmost branches. Wright designed the feature after receiving the gift of a steel beam retrieved from a dismantled aircraft carrier.

Frances Nemtin recalls that Wright especially liked to view a landscape through icicles, and he was thrilled one Thanksgiving when Taliesin experienced an ice storm, but most of the year he was satisfied to view vistas through a framework of leaves. "A tree is 50% shelter and 50% freedom," was a favourite axiom, the freedom referring to the framing effect its outspreading branches could provide, like looking at the world through a window. "He also liked big trees – like white and bur oaks – in the middle of fields, as they appear in Welsh landscapes. And he made his farm workers plough around them," Frances remembers.

Framing and veiling elements Wright admired, but in

The view from Wright's living room along a birdwalk, a narrow balcony that extends into the treetops and provides a bird's-eye view over the surrounding countryside.

FAR LEFT: A student at Taliesin harvests fresh vegetables from the kitchen garden.

LEFT: A crookneck squash growing in Wright's vegetable garden.

general he did not like vines clinging to his buildings. He preferred vines to be trained over retaining walls and atop pergolas, using numerous varieties of clematis at Taliesin and bougainvillea at Taliesin West. Vines like English ivy and Virginia creeper hid his artistry (and could be destructive of masonry and wood). "The doctor can bury his mistakes," he said. "The architect can plant vines."

Wright liked a bold splash of colour to greet visitors when they entered his valley, and so he had almost a half acre triangular bed, at the junction of route 23 and the approach road to Taliesin, planted with a mixture of petunias. "It was a good way to say *welcome*," says Frances. Today, the triangle of petunias is a memorial garden to one of Wright's most trusted associates, John deKoven Hill. Designed by Cornelia Brierly and planted in 1998 it features mostly flowering shrubs and perennials that produce decorative dried flowers or seed heads. In particular there are two massed plantings of 'Annabelle' hydrangea, the globular white flower heads turning bronze by fall; also massed plantings of *Sedum* 'Autumn Joy' (syn. 'Herbstfreude') which displays bronze seed heads until well after Christmas.

As well as assisting Wright in many of his designs, Hill managed the vegetable garden, worked at the dairy farm, looked after the two Taliesin residences, directed the Taliesin chorus, and performed classical works on the piano. In a memoir, he wrote of the effect that Wright's Taliesin had upon him (by this time Wright was married to his third wife, Olgivanna): "When I finally saw Taliesin, its impact was an emotional revelation and a tremendous shot in the arm. Here was everything I loved all real, never seen before beautiful spaces and forms, mossy stones and fountains and just enough decay here and there to add to the apparent eternal, no-time period naturalness. And here also was real 'nature' everywhere and the civilized organization of farm life right alongside and among beautiful music, elegant dinners, European films, glamorous guests, and – most remarkable of all – Mr. and Mrs. Wright, who as a couple

seemed unbelievably made for each other – handsome, stylish, quick to respond – magnetic."

Ling Po, an apprentice who wrote a memoir about his time at Taliesin, remembered how "Mr. Wright loved the richness of food and the luxuries of life. There was the dairy farm, where there was an inch of cream on the milk cans, and we churned our own butter – there was every good vegetable and fruit. Mr. Wright wanted to give all the luxuries earth can provide to nourish us, yet he always kept us in more Spartan habits."

Harison's rose (*Rosa harisonii*), an old garden variety that was a Wright favourite. He preferred wild and old-fashioned varieties to hybrids.

OPPOSITE: Midway Farm, Taliesin, and its circular, tower-like milk cooling room. The rakish spire is reminiscent of Japanese temple shrines.

BELOW: Wright admired the traditional red barns of Wisconsin, and painted his farm buildings the same warm, earthy colour. Even the Ford pick-up truck used at Midway Farm is colour-coordinated with the buildings.

Wright had strong convictions about the training architects needed. "How can an architect design without knowing the nature of wood, stone, steel and concrete?" he asked. "How can an architect design a kitchen if he has never worked in one?" Although trainees were involved in working at the Hillside Home School site, with its sleeping quarters and classroom, local masons carted sandstone from a nearby quarry and laid it under Wright's supervision. His head mason, Charlie Curtis would tell the trainees, "Boys, get the feel of the rock in your hand, or it t'aint no use." They learned to lay walls with long thin flat stones and rough edges, assorted stones protruding like a shelf at frequent intervals to create shadow patterns. Frances Nemtin wrote that as often as they laid a stone the masons would stand back to judge the effect, and Wright would smile at their enthusiasm. She heard Charlie exclaim proudly: "Ain't that the berries? Oh, saaay, h'it's a bird. Yep, she's a beauty." Wright told his students: "You are here like pebbles in a stream, grinding upon each other and shaping each other."

Frances has been manager and designer of the Taliesin flower gardens for over twenty years. She ensures that Taliesin still has plenty of summer phlox and tiger lilies since they were Wright's favourite flowers. He also admired a wild yellow rose, *Rosa harisonii*, commonly called Harison's rose. Sprays of this rose were presented to him on his birthday, June 8th, when his wife organized a big dinner party. Frequently, on these occasions, common workmen would find themselves sitting with celebrities like Adlai Stevenson, Carl Sandburg and Georgia O'Keeffe. Frances remembers that Wright was always very witty, kind and sharp. "I decided to join Taliesin in 1946 at age 23 when I was acting director at the Milwaukee Art Institute, and had mounted a Wright Exhibition," she says. After the exhibit she wondered, "What am I doing talking about art when I can be living a creative life?" She offered her services to Wright as an assistant and he hired her. Today, at age 85, she supervises the plantings at Taliesin and writes books about Wright from her vast store of knowledge. With her husband she occupies the former farm manager's house at Midway Farm, so called because it is equidistant between Taliesin and the Wright Fellowship campus, Hillside Home School complex.

57

The spillway at Taliesin that Wright designed to create a pair of lakes, which he called his water garden; it produces a beautiful 'falling cloth" waterfall. Wright planted the edges with weeping willows that will be replanted.

Between 1938 and 1947 Wright designed a complex of farm buildings primarily for his herd of Guernsey cattle. Painted red, the long low sleek buildings seem to emerge from the side of a wooded hill, like an express train leaving a tunnel. A stone milk cooling room, shaped like a silo, features a tall, sleek spire topped by a weathervane. Midway Farm and its surrounding woodland and fields create an extraordinary pastoral landscape. The rakish spire piercing the sky and bean fields contoured below it resemble a Shinto shrine surrounded by rice paddies. The buildings are in perfect scale to their surroundings. Moreover, the red barn siding is echoed in the body paint of a Ford truck that is usually parked beside the milk cooling tower.

Wright's admiration for red barns in the landscape is evident from statements he made about the painter, Georgia O'Keeffe. Like Wright, O'Keeffe was born in Wisconsin just fifty miles east of Taliesin, and though she spent most of her adult life in New York City and New Mexico, she returned to Wisconsin to paint. "The red barn is one of Wisconsin's greatest assets in her landscape," he wrote in his *Autobiography*. Five years after her paintings of red barns in Wisconsin, O'Keeffe was invited by Wright to lecture at the Taliesin Fellowship; he even offered to build her a house on the property. But it was an invitation she could not accept because of her busy life.

The wooden spire atop the stone milk cooling tower at Midway Farm is echoed in a similar structure Wright designed for the entrance to his valley. Originally designed as a restaurant, the structure now serves as the Visitor's Center. It has low, sleek lines similar to those of Midway Farm, and overlooks a wide expanse of the Wisconsin River. Viewed from a concrete bridge that crosses the river to connect Taliesin with Spring Green, the red spire produces an impression of Japan even more strongly than Midway Farm, particularly the way the entire structure is set in a verdant hillside, with just the tower and spire visible through the billowing trees. When the sun sets beyond the bridge, with Taliesin in the background, the colours of the sky and water are glorious.

Wright valued the mirror effect that a large body of still water can produce, and so he dammed a creek that ran

BELOW TOP: Hillside Home School, Taliesin. The Wright-designed complex is a teaching facility for the Frank Lloyd Wright Fellowship.

BELOW BOTTOM: The workroom at Hillside Home School, a design inspired by Wright's walking through a nearby pine forest.

below the house to create what he describes on his plans as a water garden. A stone spillway backs up the water for a lake and creates a beautiful sheet of falling water, in an expression the Japanese call "falling cloth". The spillway is built into a rock shelf, and a fall of boulders helps to break up the wide expanse of stonework. The lake adds much more than a mirror. It provides a source of water for the courtyard fountains, and helps irrigate the orchard, vineyard and vegetable gardens. "The mirror is seen in Nature in the surface of lakes in the hollows of the mountains and in the pools deep in the shadows of the trees," he wrote in his *Autobiography*. "In winding ribbons . . . the rivers . . . catch and give back the flying birds, clouds and blue sky. A dreary thing to have that element leave the landscape."

Wright loved the weeping willow tree as it was an important element of Japanese gardens and he rimmed the lake with them, to suggest grace and tranquillity. Like the Japanese, he considered architecture and landscaping "frozen music". He likened trees to beautiful buildings. "The secret of all styles of architecture was the same secret that gave *character* to trees," he wrote. Between the weeping willows, clumps of hardy swamp hibiscus bloom from midsummer to autumn, their dinner-plate size flowers in white, pink and red, and masses of thistles producing silky thistledown that drifts over the water like a summer snowstorm.

Hillside was the location of Wright's grandfather's original house, and it had become a co-educational boarding school, Hillside Home School – run by two aunts, Nell and Jane Lloyd-Jones. Every spring the children gathered wild violets and packed them in boxes to be sent to hospitals in Chicago and Milwaukee. The two aunts took a vow never to marry, and to devote their lives to the school. Wright acquired the school after his aunts closed it in 1914, later adding a drafting studio and dormitory rooms for students. The design for the drafting studio is inspired by his walking through a pine forest, the pillars representing trunks of trees, and the cross members representing a criss-crossed overhead branch pattern.

In 1933, at Hillside Home School, Wright added a theatre for musical and theatrical performances. Wright himself designed a curtain that screens the stage as an

A stage curtain at Hillside Home School designed by Wright. It is an abstract representation of the countryside around Taliesin.

abstraction of the landscape at Taliesin. Cubist swatches of fabric are woven to create the colourful pattern in a mostly green, black and red motif, similar to the cubist brushstrokes employed by the great French Impressionist, Cézanne and the modernist, Picasso.

Most of Wright's designs were inspired by elements in nature, though it was sometimes difficult to see exactly where the inspiration came from. For example, at Taliesin West, the idea of using canvas canopies to roof a similar drafting studio came from Wright's observation of membranes within the trunk of a saguaro cactus and then seeing sheep herders tents in a nearby valley.

In 1898, at age 29, Wright designed the Romeo & Juliet windmill to pump water to the Hillside Home School. Local farmers predicted the windmill would fall in a wind, but it outlived all the sceptics, mainly because of Wright's shape for the foundation — a fusion of a hexagon and diamond. In Wright's mind's eye the hexagon (Romeo) embraced the diamond (Juliet), hence the name Romeo and Juliet. Below the windmill Frances Nemtin has restored a portion of prairie that had become overgrown. She cleared the slope

and seeded it with prairie wildflowers. It has come back every year.

The windmill overlooks another historic building, Tan-Y-Deri (Welsh for "under the oaks"), a home that Wright designed for a sister, Jane Porter, in 1907. The house features leaded diamond-paned windows that seem to echo the cross-hatching on a nearby ancient silver maple tree. A hiking trail leads from Tan-Y-Deri down to the Hillside Home School campus, its entire length roofed over by the branches of native trees like the vaulted columns of a cathedral.

Frances recalls numerous changes to the landscape at Taliesin, mostly with respect to tree plantings. A number of mature weeping willows that rimmed the lakes have been lost to storms and beavers, and it will take time for new plantings to mature. A champion elm that dominated the corner of route 23 and the Taliesin approach road, fell victim to Dutch elm disease, and was replaced by a disease-resistant elm. Though storms continually topple mature pines and oaks, they are systematically replaced with younger stock. The saddest loss for the Taliesin community was a giant bur oak with wide spreading cantilevered branches at the

An archive photograph of the upper courtyard at Taliesin before a severe storm in 1998 toppled the trees and changed the site from shady to sunny.

centre of a gathering place Wright called the Tea Circle. It shaded much of the front garden and its demise required a change in the flowerbeds, from predominantly shade-loving plants like hostas and impatiens, to those that are happy in sun, such as dahlias and nicotiana. Perhaps the most significant change has been Taliesin's official organic certification. Many volunteers help to maintain the gardens under Frances's direction. Fifteen are involved in putting the gardens to bed at the end of October, removing spent plants and laying mulch. They return in spring at the end of April to assess winter's depredations and prepare the beds for new plantings.

Paradise lost and found

It was a warm, blue-sky mid-summer day, on Saturday August 15, 1914. The garden shimmered from the bold colours of perennials; hummingbirds whirred among the nectar-rich orange flower clusters of trumpet creeper;

bees from Wright's own beehives buzzed among massive clumps of pink and red summer phlox, and monarch butterflies from the surrounding meadows hovered above the fragrant pink monarda. Wright himself was in Chicago, supervising finishing touches to his Midway Gardens project, a restaurant and entertainment complex. Mamah Cheney, his live-in companion, occupied herself for most of the morning, organizing photographs and drawings for an exhibit of Wright's work in San Francisco. She ordered lunch on a screened porch off the living quarters with her two young children, John (12) and Martha (8).

Wright received news of a fire at Taliesin while making finishing touches to a wall mural with his son John. A taxi was called to take them to the station to catch a train for Spring Green.

The three-hour train ride for Wright became a nightmare. At every station newspaper reporters waited on the platform, and informed Wright that in addition to

FAR LEFT: The white, tubular flowers of ornamental tobacco (*Nicotiana*) shimmer above the upper courtyard at Taliesin, with the guest wing in the background.

LEFT: Red dahlias, one of the flowers that filled Mamah Cheney's casket, in the upper courtyard, their colours harmonising with the shades of the house behind.

a fire, there were fatalities. Wright's son later recalled the journey to hell: "I have often tried to erase from my mind the anguish that was in Dad's face in that feebly lighted compartment; when he learned the ghastly details from the reporters and heard them shouted from the throats of newsboys: *Taliesin Burned to the Ground. Seven Slain.*"

The dead included Mamah, her two children and five workers, murdered by a house servant who went berserk.

After observing the still burning shell from the road, and noting the sad sight of its blackened chimneys silhouetted against the moonlit sky, Wright spent the night at Tan-Y-Deri, and in the morning walked among the still smouldering ruins with a Chicago Tribune reporter.

A crushed dahlia flower attracted his attention and seemed to raise his spirits. He picked the flower and stirred the earth around its roots to give the plant a new lease of life. He then cast a last backward glance at the devastation, and walked away.

Wright gathered all the flowers he could salvage from the garden and made piles of dinner-plate dahlias, summer phlox, long-stemmed zinnias, and armloads of peppery-scented nasturtiums. He ordered a deep grave to be dug at Unity Chapel, and filled the casket with flowers to make a floral bed for Mrs. Cheney. Her body was laid on this and Wright sprinkled more flowers on top of her. By late afternoon the casket was loaded onto a horse-drawn cart and a small group of mourners followed it to the graveyard for burial.

After an agonizing period of mourning, Wright looked to his work for hope and healing. "I could feel now only in terms of rebuilding," he said. "I could get relief from a kind of continuous nausea, by work . . . In action there is release from anguish of mind."

***

Wright planted a pine tree over Mrs. Cheney's grave, today marked by a simple stone plaque, in the graveyard at Unity Church, within sight of Taliesin.

Flowerbeds, green lawns and a collection of native yucca in the forecourt at Taliesin West. Rising behind the low, elongated buildings lit by an early morning sunrise are the McDowell Mountains of the Sonoran Desert.

3 TALIESIN WEST, Wright's winter home (1937)

In 1937, five years after Wright established his apprenticeship program at Taliesin, known as the Taliesin Fellowship, he purchased six hundred acres of Sonoran Desert at Scottsdale, Arizona, to further his architectural teaching and also to provide an escape from Wisconsin's harsh winters.

He discovered the site, with the McDowell Mountain range in the background, while consulting on the design of the Biltmore Hotel, in nearby Phoenix. The real estate agent warned him that the land was virtually worthless, because there was no water on the property, but Wright's instinct told him that if he dug deep enough he would find water; and he was correct. The view, he declared, "Is like looking over the rim of the world." Nothing interfered with the pristine image of raw desert and cradle of distant mountains.

In his *Autobiography*, Wright wrote about his decision to gain a foothold in the Sonora Desert: "There was something everlasting, fundamental and worth clinging to here. Barely eking out an existence in the desert, the saguaro cactus, the cholla, and bignonia stood at a sculptural scale, taller and nobler than man. It was another Eden . . . A grand garden the like of which in sheer beauty of space and pattern does not exist, I think, in the world."

What Wright found to excite him in this pure desert landscape were plants with architectural forms, not only cacti but also trees with tortuous limbs, like the mesquite. "The spiritual cathartic that was the desert . . . swept the spirit clean of stagnant ways and habitual forms ready for fresh adventure," he wrote in an article for *Arizona Highways* magazine. "A struggle against nature never appealed to me," he said. "The struggle for and with Nature thrilled me and inspired my work."

In the desert he wanted his work "To grow more simple; more expressive with fewer lines, fewer forms; more articulate with less labour . . . more fluent, although more

The triangular reflecting pool
serves both as a decorative
water feature and a
swimming pool.

coherent; more organic." Defending his desert architecture, with its bold, clean lines, Wright exclaimed: "Plainness is not simplicity . . . Nine pounds where three are sufficient is obesity. But to eliminate expressive words in speaking or writing — words that *intensify* or vivify meaning — is not simplicity. Nor is similar elimination in architecture."

Taliesin West faces Paradise Valley. Most of its construction was achieved by apprentices who camped nearby in temporary tents and hauled rocks and boulders out of the desert for building. They even constructed special cradles in order to move large plants, like the giant saguaro cactus, to decorate the site as living sculpture, placing them where Wright directed.

Cornelia Brierly was one of the first apprentices to arrive at Taliesin West when it was a bare site. She lived in a tent for three years until the permanent structures were built. Wright insisted that every indigenous desert plant disturbed by the construction be set aside in a special nursery area. He later moved these into raised planters or to new homes beyond the boundary walls.

The direction of prevailing winds, the movement of the sun and Wright's desire for particular shadow patterns to fall across his terraces helped him to decide on an east-west alignment of the main buildings, and the prominent triangular trajectory of a substantial gravel terrace that projects into the desert like the prow of a ship.

The different areas of the building — the workroom, apartments, main living area and accommodation for faculty, are linked by courtyards, patios, garden spaces and an 86-foot pergola which creates a, shady, verdant corridor the entire length of the workroom. A stone retaining wall marks the boundary between architectural space and desert wilderness, providing a raised view over Paradise Valley. It also serves as a barrier against intrusion by unwelcome desert creatures, particularly rattlesnakes.

Crucial to Wright's design is a rectangular green lawn, as soft as velvet and as green as a billiard table. Kept lush by irrigation, it is in stark contrast to the harsh brown landscape of mountains and stony desert soil. Wright liked to walk across this green carpet in his bare feet, with early morning dew still on the grass.

The sunset terrace, on the west side of Wright's living room, is a spacious textured concrete apron able to accommodate large gatherings. As an ornamental accent, it features a pedestal that supports three large dishes filled with coloured glass balls resembling small balloons. Wright loved colourful balloons and often featured circular shapes in glass panels and wall murals.

Wright later re-aligned the sunset terrace to avoid looking at power lines that the local power company refused to bury underground. Wright's living room — called the Garden Room — has one side facing an enclosed lawn with a

ABOVE FAR LEFT: The silky yellow flowers of a prickly pear cactus (*Opuntia*) from the Sonoran Desert contrast with vibrant red blooms of a red bougainvillea vine.

ABOVE LEFT: The spiky foliage of *Agave striata* resembles a sea urchin in a raised planter at Taliesin West.

ABOVE: The poker-like flowers of *Aloe vera* thrust skyward like rockets through a thicket of prickly pear cactus.

ABOVE: A Saguaro cactus forms a sculptural pillar in a raised planter. The spiky foliage of a Joshua tree rises above the red pergola in the background.
LEFT: An overall view of the middle level courtyard.

BELOW: The main terrace features three copper dishes with clusters of coloured glass balls as a focal point.

red moongate set into the far wall; and another side looking out into the raw desert. Entrance to the Garden Room is through a low portal set between thick stone walls, like the entrance to a Mayan temple.

A bell tower, with triangular supports for the bell, is perched above the drafting studio, its pointed outline echoing the jagged peaks of the McDowell Mountains to the northeast. To the southwest the drafting studio looks out onto a broad sunken garden terrace and pool that projects far out into the desert. Along the northeast side of the drafting studio are views over a raised terraced garden of desert plants, the McDowell Mountains visible in the distance.

The pergola that runs the entire length of the drafting studio, creates a pleasant shaded transition from the sunny forecourt to the brightly lit drafting room, establishing the sense of compression and release that Wright liked to create both inside and outside his buildings. The pergola was originally planted with tall chain-fruit prickly pear, but as visitors kept injuring themselves on the spines, it was planted with bougainvillea that blooms intermittently throughout the year. Although bougainvillea does have spines, it is not nearly as injurious as cacti.

Wright taught his students to take inspiration from being in the open air. He explained that his best ideas came to him from working outdoors, spending time in the garden. He never tired of teaching apprentices how to use garden tools. Apprentice Roger D'Astous, now a well-known Quebec architect, recalled how time spent gardening involved more than deadheading petunias. Apprentices and teachers alike shared outdoor work, with discussions about architecture usually the topic of conversation while gardening. Wright taught his women students how to use a saw and a pick to avoid straining themselves. Another student recalled how Wright took time to show how to weed flower beds, and how to recognise the difference between weeds with surface roots that are easily pulled, and those with tenacious tap roots that need prying out of the ground so they will not grow back.

Initially, Wright wanted Taliesin West planted only with indigenous desert plants, but the injuries that

The view from the Garden Room – Wright's living room – at Taliesin West, across a green lawn to a moongate. Wright liked to walk in bare feet on the grass when it was covered in early morning dew.

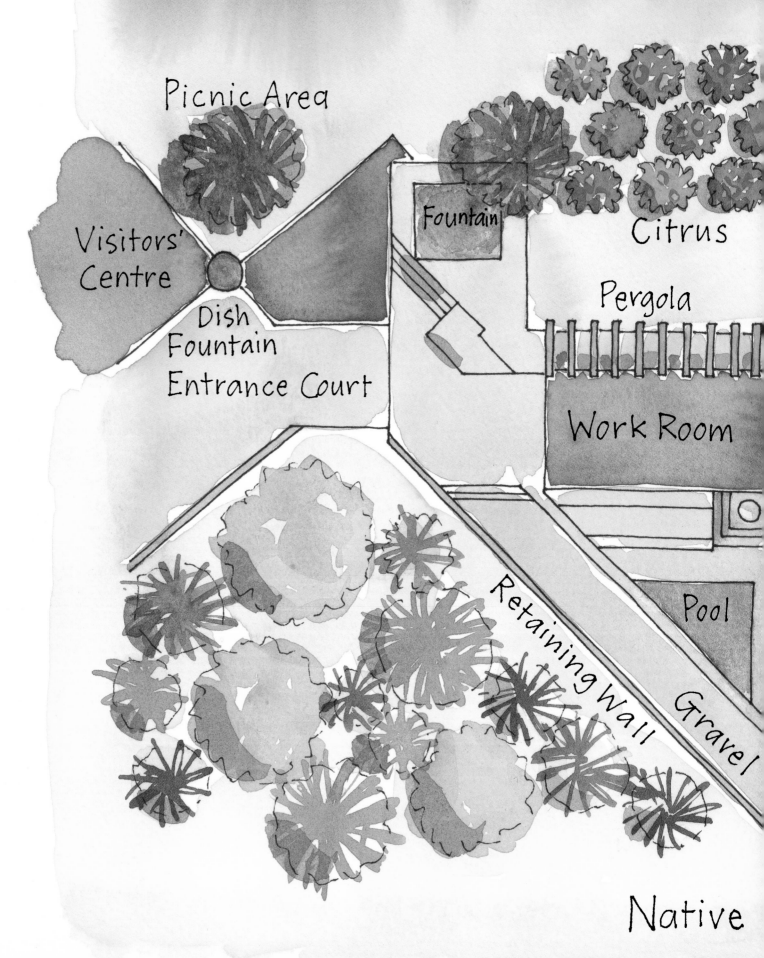

An outline plan of
Taliesin West.

Foothills of the McDowell Mountains

Picnic Area

Visitors' Centre

Fountain

Citrus

Pergola

Dish
Fountain
Entrance Court

Work Room

Pool

Retaining Wall

Gravel

Native

Orchard

Dry
Stream

Pool

Loggia

LivingQuarters

Garden
Room

Green Garden

Patio

Desert
garden

Lawn

Court

Desert

Although Wright generally disliked his architecture being hidden by exuberant foundation plantings, at Taliesin West portions of the base of the buildings are planted with bushy shrubs, such as bougainvillea and firethorn (*Pyracantha*), seen here in flower, as they help to anchor the building to the desert landscape.

BELOW: A hedge of bougainvillea cascades down a retaining wall beneath Wright's pergola at Taliesin West.

BOTTOM: A kinetic fountain designed by Wright. Glass balls inside the dome produce the sound of chimes.

apprentices suffered from thoughtlessly rubbing against them, caused him to reconsider and allow some exotics inside the compound. Today there is even a mature rubber plant and orchid trees from Brazil. Cornelia remembers when Taliesin had a fine palm collection, but when these grew large Wright considered them out of scale with their surroundings, and had them all removed.

'We stuck to desert plants beyond the footprint of the building," notes Cornelia. "Integrated grassy carpets, smooth steps and terrace surfaces, pools of water, and the kinetic effect of fountains also are part of the contrasts to the rugged textures of the desert."

Wright liked to place vertical accents in locations where they would provide contrast to the predominantly horizontal lines of the buildings. From the desert, in addition to the giant saguaro cactus, he brought in upright evergreens, and even narrow, elongated stones from the mountains, upended to form a plinth. Cornelia also remembers how Wright strove to integrate his buildings with the natural landscape. "This integration begins at ground level," she says. "With the broad gravel paths and courtyards matching the desert floor, and the roof angles echoing in an abstract way the background mountains. Both muted and brightly coloured desert rock in what we called battered rubble walls . . . reappear in painted surfaces, sculptures, oriental pottery and American Indian art."

Where Taliesin, Wisconsin, is cool, green, lush, and tranquil, and the contours in the surrounding countryside are smooth, Taliesin West is harsh, brown, dry and hot. "I have always regarded the desert as the greatest lesson in construction," Wright wrote. "Form following function if you like – or form and function being one. The saguaro is the greatest example of a skyscraper that was ever built."

Wright also admired and respected the prickly chollas, "This beautiful blonde of the desert that is as wicked as anything that has ever existed," he explained. "It has little fish hooks for foliage that will get at you if you don't watch out. They call it the jumping cholla because as you pass by, the slightest movement will cause this marvellous little hedgehog to impale itself on your leg."

He told his apprentices that he considered the Sonoran Desert the youngest landscape in the United States.

LEFT: A Bauhinia tree and bougainvillea shade the almost hidden entrance to the staff annex.

BELOW: An elegant garden gate designed by Wright provides access to the gardens of the staff annex.

Billowing shapes of
bougainvillea and brittlebush
(*Encelia farinosa*) decorate
the staff annex courtyard.

"California is old," he said. "almost worn smooth. The curves are like those of a bald-headed man, but here everything is fresh, original, edges pretty much preserved, erosion still going on at a terrific rate, making chasms. It is extraordinarily picturesque, probably newer than anything, and nearer to the original catastrophe than anything I know."

He exhorted his apprentices to avoid spending their free time downtown, but to spend it hiking through the desert. "The desert has produced all this marvellous growth, which is all armed. There isn't a thing in the desert that isn't armed . . . everywhere you go you get prodded, stuck, cut, torn . . . if you interfere with any of it. So the best thing is . . . to just look at it, and admire it because it does achieve a beautiful synthesis of form."

In particular he wanted the apprentices to look for dramatic contrasts."A cactus is a bloom beyond any bloom, I think manufactured by plants anywhere in the world. And there you have an interesting syllogism . . . the desperate nature of the armed plant and the exquisite beautiful inflorescence it produces...so here you have a chance to see things, to learn the art of seeing, which of course is another form of being."

Nature trails meander out from the courtyards of Taliesin West to the foothills, connecting the apprentice shelters and passing a tea circle situated below a large rock fall. Several of the shelters also incorporate tea circles. Cornelia Brierly, reminiscing about her walks through the desert, wrote: "In a year when moisture is plentiful Taliesin West and the mountains beyond luxuriate in a beautiful desert garden. The yellow daisy flowers – pots of gold of our desert – of the yellow brittle bush, bloom profusely come spring. The palo verde trees glow with lemon yellow flowers. A golden poppy field around the curve of the mountain is interspersed with blue lupine and wild onion."

D'Astous recalls a photograph of ten apprentices rolling a massive boulder with pictographs into place as a garden accent, Wright directing its placement. "This is a symbol of what a master he is," said D'Astous, and how a strong *esprit de corps* allowed the Fellowship to work together, on the same wavelength. "Time spent landscaping produced its

LEFT: Wide, pyramid-like steps, redolent of Mayan imagery, overlook the pool and lead to the entrance to the Work Room. The boulder, placed as a sculptural accent, has petroglyphs (pictographs) on its surface, and was discovered in the desert.

OVERLEAF: Sunset at Taliesin West viewed from the forecourt, with silhouettes of saguaro cactus Wright transplanted to enhance his view.

rewards," he said. "Even doing flower arrangements when we were assigned dining room duty, was a way to express composition and a sensitivity to materials."

Wright believed that to be a successful architect one must develop poise and social skills in order to win a client's trust. So his wife Olgivanna planned black tie events such as formal dinners that often featured plays, movies and music performed in a special theatre. One apprentice, Jim Shildroth, who came from a working class family, valued the emphasis placed on social graces since he could put them to good use when entertaining affluent clients from upper-class backgrounds later in his career. "The formal dinners and the dress-up evenings, and the special guests that we were able to mingle with ... were very special to me."

Another graduate recalled that the Taliesin West lifestyle was like living in a court in Europe, back in the days of royalty, " ... where you had musicians in residence and all sorts of wonderful activities that even wealthy people did not have."

Canadian violinist Harry Adaskin, following a visit to the two Taliesins, wrote in a memoir: "For people like ourselves who knew nothing of architecture, it was extremely interesting to watch Mr. Wright directing his apprentices to making improvements to buildings and the gardens and the general landscape: the meticulous placing of bushes and trees and all the thousand and one things an architect must know and be master of. Even the arrangements of flowers for the dinner tables were given careful scrutiny for the best combination of colours and shape, so that the final effect, like a passage in Beethoven, looked inevitable. And because it was inevitable, it looked disarmingly easy as well as beautiful."

First-year apprentices at Taliesin West generally lived in simple eight-by-eight foot square tents, but later they were encouraged to design and build more elaborate shelters or enlarge existing ones, and this practice remains today. Sleeping in the desert in these simple shelters not only introduces the apprentices to the distinctive sounds and sights of the desert, but gives them first-hand experience of integrating a building unobtrusively with its surroundings.

These tiny structures, often one room combining a living and sleeping area, dot the desert surrounding Taliesin West. It's all part of the "learning by doing" concept

RIGHT: A claret cup cactus in one of the planters at Taliesin West.

BELOW: An apprentice shelter tucked into the side of a ravine, a short walk from the main building of Taliesin West. Wright applauded designs that intruded least on the dramatic, pristine desert landscape.

OPPOSITE: A dish fountain at the entrance to Taliesin West spills re-circulated water into a basin, with one of Wright's *Sprite* statues in the background.

Wright insisted upon. By living in the desert, first in a tent, then designing a desert shelter, the apprentices discovered how to make architecture part of the indigenous landscape. Wright himself lived in a canvas tent while working on his first Arizona commission, and found the canvas to be such a good roofing material for the desert, he incorporated it into his workshop at Taliesin. He wrote of this revelation: "The white luminous canvas overhead and canvas used instead of window glass afforded such an agreeable diffusion of light within, was so enjoyable and sympathetic to the desert, that I now felt more than ever oppressed by the thought of the opaque solid overhead of the much too solid Mid-western house."

As well as designing their own shelters, apprentices are encouraged to landscape around them. As a consequence they learn what plants will thrive in a dry landscape, and how to provide irrigation for more common garden plants.

Wright also placed great importance in organized tours to other parts of the desert, primarily so apprentices could be exposed to new natural configurations as inspiration for their designs. New patterns provided by desert plants, unusual rock formations, even the bleached bones of desert animals, all provided stimulus for creative design, in the same way that the bleached bones of cattle inspired the famous paintings of Georgia O'Keeffe when she moved to New Mexico.

4 FALLINGWATER, (1935)

In the bucolic Laurel Highlands of Pennsylvania, some sixty miles south-east of Pittsburgh, are three outstanding Wright residences close to each other, and all three are open to the public. The most famous is Fallingwater, a weekend retreat with servants' quarters and an adjacent guest house, built for Pittsburgh department store owners the Edgar J. Kaufmann family over a series of waterfalls along Bear Run. (The second Wright residence, Kentuck Knob, is described in chapter 7; a third, the Duncan House, is described on page 154 in the list of Wright's sites open for public tours).

The main living area of Wright's Fallingwater and master bedroom terrace are cantilevered dramatically over a roaring waterfall. Key to the success of Wright's design is the waterfall itself and rock shelves that descend steeply along a wooded ravine. The family had picnicked at the ravine and when they hired Wright they imagined a residence facing the creek to give them an exhilarating view of the falls. Wright deliberated a long time before putting pencil to paper, and began drafting his conceptual plan for Fallingwater just three hours before Mr. and Mrs. Kaufmann arrived at Taliesin for a review of his proposals. His design broke one of his steadfast rules, that of situating his residences to provide the occupants with the best possible view, but his plan for Fallingwater – in favour of presenting a more spectacular view of the house and falls from downstream – was quickly agreed to.

From 1925 to 1934 Wright had few commissions owing to the Depression and the general belief that his work was behind the times. He was deeply in debt and needed a stunning success to jump-start his career. In 1937, when Fallingwater was completed, the project provided the necessary publicity and critical acclaim to make his final twenty years the most productive of his life. Fallingwater, more than any other project, established him firmly as a great architect – an innovator instead of a has-been.

A half-mile, snaking driveway leads to the house from the main road, through mostly deciduous forest of towering sugar maples and an understorey of native dogwoods, redbuds and wild rhododendron. The residence itself is revealed only at the last moment, when the veil of indigenous trees thins out along the ravine. Seemingly embedded into a knuckle of rock, Wright described his building as "An extension of the cliff, shaped to the music of the stream."

The driveway crosses the stream by a broad flat-span bridge, to a forecourt where the main entrance is inconspicuous and almost hidden, like the entrance to a cave. Beyond, a steep wooded hillside creates a leafy backdrop that changes dramatically with the seasons. In spring,

OPPOSITE, ABOVE LEFT & ABOVE RIGHT: Fallingwater in winter, autumn and spring.

Viewed from the opposite bank of the Bear Run stream, the cantilevered balconies at Fallingwater jut out into and become part of the enveloping woodland.

Fallingwater's living room balcony and its view downstream. The steps at the right lead to the stream bed and a plunge pool in the bed-rock.

among bright green newly unfurled foliage, the blossoms of white dogwood rise into the leafy canopy like flocks of butterflies. At this time the waterfalls usually run full force with a thunderous sound, from abundant spring rains and snow melt. The dark greens of summer are punctuated with the bright pinks of late-blooming rhododendron blossoms, while in autumn the sugar maples over the house make a cathedral of russet colours – molten reds, buttercup yellows and flame orange. But all this pales to the effect that winter can produce, when freezing cold turns the waterfalls to ice and snowfall accentuates the rounded forms of boulders and the network of tree trunks and bare branches.

Considering the hand that nature has played in the setting, one may wonder what landscape innovation could be attributed to Wright. Perhaps Carla Lind, author of *Frank Lloyd Wright's Fallingwater* (Pomegranate), explained it best when she wrote, "If Fallingwater is viewed as a perfect marriage of building and site, the leading partner is nature . . . The retreat was rooted in the earth, dipped into the stream, looked into the treetops, stretched out like branches from a tree, and used nature's own colour palette."

Without doubt, it is the artful way Wright dovetailed his design for human shelter into a pristine natural environment that makes Fallingwater iconoclastic and a landscaping triumph. At Fallingwater, it is the brilliant – and revolutionary – placement of the house itself that constitutes the landscaping. Wright's design makes the building part of the landscape, one of the elements of the garden. They are organically intertwined, with the stream and waterfalls constantly heard inside the house as they run underneath.

Fallingwater exemplifies Wright's credo for good landscaping, when he wrote: "It is wrong to think that landscaping is a collection of specimens from all parts of the world . . . The finding of plant varieties is a scientific venture, fine and noble in itself, but it must not be confused with art, as is so often done. To be inspired by and to create parks and gardens out of the beauty and composition of our native landscape is a much higher accomplishment than to form a garden with varieties of plants that have no intimate association with each other or with us and which at best

91

The plunge pool next to a guest cottage at Fallingwater, with native dogwoods (*Cornus florida*) and redbuds (*Cercis canadensis*) in bloom.

become a mere patch work influenced by the curious and scientific mind."

At Fallingwater Wright knew how important it was to save as many existing natural features as possible. Even the topmost boulder of the main promontory projects into the living room to form a hearth for the fireplace, a suggestion of Kaufmann's he readily agreed to. Yet he did make some subtle touches of exterior landscape design, particularly between the main residence and a guest cottage. They include terraces above the main residence for a massed planting of native Christmas ferns that slopes down to a cliff edging the driveway. A breezeway of beams creates a slatted pergola-like structure, so that part of the cliff is shaded for healthy moss and fern growth, and part is in sunlight, making a sunny rockery, bright with native blue forget-me-nots (*Myosotis sylvatica*), and hardy native

geranium (*Geranium maculatum*) in spring. A stepped covered walkway, overhung with redbuds and dogwoods, connects the guest cottage to the main house.

The terraces also allowed the Kaufmanns to grow some cultivated plants, like lilies, that still bloom in summer beside a plunge pool off a sunny flagstone patio beside the guest cottage. A Japanese white wisteria covers an arbour attached to the guest cottage to add an oriental flavour. The trellis beams across the driveway leading uphill from the main residence provide the "compression and release" sensation that Wright favoured for both interior and exterior spaces.

One ingenious outdoor feature Wright incorporated into his Fallingwater design, is accessible through a glass hatch in the living room floor. It leads down a flight of steps to the creek bed where he installed a plunge pool among the

boulders beside the stream. Fed by spring water, it is too cold to use in winter, but it was a favourite place for the Kaufmanns to cool off in summer.

Since the exterior woodland is so beautiful, whether one looks up into the leaf canopy, out to the hillsides or downstream, the sense of being in the treetops is profound. And so Wright paid special attention to the design and placement of windows. The spaciousness of the main rooms is extended outdoors by means of wide, linear windows, framing the leaf patterns of trees as though they are mosaics. Particularly ingenious are corner windows with red frames, hinged at the sides to open out and offer an even wider unrestricted view of the verdant scenery. Other corners feature invisible glass seams to create the illusion that no window exists there at all.

Fallingwater is the only Wright-designed residence open

to the public with its furnishings and art collections intact. Edgar Kaufmann jr. gave Fallingwater to the Western Pennsylvania Conservancy in 1963, and it is the only site in their care with a significant historic building. Kaufmann believed that the Conservancy was the best choice to ensure Fallingwater's future because it was "devoted to the salutary and encompassing values of human life in touch with nature." Other sites administered by the Conservancy are mostly natural areas such as parks, according to Lynda S. Waggoner, Director of Fallingwater.

The building itself recently experienced a major renovation, requiring $3,000,000 to strengthen Wright's main cantilevered terrace, which was sinking into the stream. A further $8,000,000 was needed to install public water and a sewage treatment plant to accommodate the influx of visitors. "We're happy to have such a heavy capital

A stepped covered walkway leads from the guest cottage to the main house, bordering a slope planted with native rhododendron, ferns and a graceful redbud tree.

ABOVE: A canopy bordering the guest house is decorated with a white wisteria vine, one of a few non-native plants at Fallingwater.

RIGHT: Trellis beams span the driveway, partly covering a rockery planted with moss, ferns, native geraniums (*Geranium maculatum*) and bright blue forget-me-nots (*Myosotis sylvatica*). This slatted structure connects the main house with a steep slope leading to servants' and guest quarters.

expenditure behind us," said Lynda Waggoner. "Now I want to concentrate on getting the landscape the way I'd like to see it."

Though Fallingwater is in a breathtaking forest setting, with towering sugar maples and an under-planting of native *Rhododendron maximum* bordering the stream and waterfalls, she wants to introduce more native plants. "The woodland used to be thick with white native dogwood," she explains. "But the dogwood declined as a result of a fungus disease. Now, it seems to have developed a resistance, so I'd like to see more dogwoods planted."

Also, she would like to enhance approach roads beyond the property planted with dogwoods and redbuds and other native flowering trees, "So that visitors can sense the presence of Fallingwater as soon as they enter the valley." Another desire is for a richer assortment of native wildflowers since the Laurel Highlands are a prime habitat for colonies of trillium, Virginia bluebells, blue woodland phlox, lady's-slipper orchids and winterberry. Along the woodland paths she envisages a wider assortment of native mosses and ferns, the presence of the stream providing a cool, moist environment in which to thrive.

With few exceptions, introduced plants like bugle weed and English ivy are being eradicated. An exception is the mature white Japanese wisteria on a wall of the adjacent guest residence. It will be retained since it adds an oriental aura to Wright's design, which is inspired by Japanese architecture. However, Lynda acknowledged that it is invasive and to stop its spreading into unwanted areas, it is now stripped of its seed pods before they have a chance to ripen. Another exception is being made for the colony of oriental lilies beside the upper plunge pool because the Kaufmann family planted them there.

"Wright made no specific recommendations for planting Fallingwater since he could not envision anything more beautiful than the natural woodland with its waterfalls, and so we strive to maintain that philosophy," Lynda explained.

"A struggle against nature never appealed to me," Wright concluded. "The struggle for and with Nature thrilled me and inspired my work."

"Fallingwater is Wright's most powerful piece of structural drama. It is the most sublime integration of man and nature," wrote the New York Times.

FAR LEFT, LEFT & BELOW: Native wildflowers at Fallingwater: great white trillium (*Trillium grandiflorum*), Virginia bluebells, (*Mertensia virginica*) and pink lady's-slipper orchids (*Cypripedium acaule*).

" I am an abstractionist seeking the pattern behind the realism. "

WRIGHT TO JENS JENSON

5 WRIGHT'S GARDEN SCULPTURE

Throughout his professional life Wright considered architecture the "mother art", while music, painting and sculpture were embellishments. For his first home in Oak Park, he commissioned Richard Bock to create two sets of distinctive sculptures. They include a matched pair of muscular nude men in a crouched position above the entrance to his studio, as though struggling to escape invisible chains. Called *The Boulders* – probably for the likeness each has to a piece of canyon stone polished by wind and water – the pink toned pieces stand as sentinels at opposite ends of the front portico. These are concrete replicas of the originals that are believed to have deteriorated over the years and have since been lost. Bock also carved a set of four stork images for the entrance columns supporting the front portico and the *Boulder* sculptures above. The storks represent "wise birds", flanked by a tree of knowledge, a book of learning and a scroll whose meaning is a puzzle, but may represent the record of human endeavour.

Wright continued to design sculpture whenever a commission called for one. He also designed wall murals, outdoor planters, furnishings and stained glass work for windows. Perhaps his most famous sculpture is entitled *The Flower in the Crannied Wall*, a collaboration between Wright and Bock, showing a beautiful neo-classical female nude examining an abstract of a Wright skyscraper. The words to the Tennyson poem of the same name are inscribed on the back of the statue. Produced for the entryway to the Dana House, in Springfield, Illinois, the original piece stands five-and-a-half feet tall, and is cast in terracotta. Wright liked the statue so much he had a white plaster cast made of it, and mounted the sculpture on a wall above the entrance courtyard at Taliesin. Over the years, however, the harsh Wisconsin winters caused considerable damage, including the loss of both her arms, like the *Venus de Milo*. Today, the sculpture is under cover, sheltered within a stairwell

leading from the upper courtyard at Taliesin to the Hill Wing, above the Tea Circle. An estimated $40,000 is needed to restore it.

For his Midway Gardens commission – a restaurant and entertainment complex on Chicago's south side – Wright designed scores of life-size, highly stylized statues for surmounting walls and pedestals, like those in a Greek temple. A series known as *Sprites* was the result of collaboration between Wright and a young immigrant Italian sculptor, Alfonso Iannelli. The two most endearing are of women with geisha-like hairstyles, titled *Meditating Sprite* and *Smiling Sprite*, each blending German art deco and eighteenth century Japanese artistic expression.

When Midway Gardens was demolished in 1929, many of its sculptures were used as fill for a breakwater along Chicago's Lake Shore Drive. However, the demolition

OPPOSITE: *The Flower in the Crannied Wall*, a sculpture designed in collaboration with sculptor Richard Bock. Once a garden ornament at Taliesin, it now occupies a stairwell to protect it from the elements.

BELOW: A pair of dish planters designed by Wright for the entrance to his Oak Park studio, with one of *The Boulder* sculptures behind.

97

FAR LEFT: A pair of *Sprites* used as garden accents at the Arizona Biltmore Hotel, Phoenix, where Wright worked as a consulting architect.

LEFT: A *Sprite* in the green garden at Taliesin West faces a bougainvillea vine.

BELOW: A sculpture by former Wright apprentice Heloise Crista, entitled *Wind Jammers*, used as a garden accent at Taliesin West.

BELOW BOTTOM: A replica of Wright's sculpture *Nakomis* at Taliesin West. Wright designed the original to honour the Plains Indians whose culture he admired.

contractor, William Newman, saved a few pieces and sold them to a Wright client, Mrs. Helen Raab, who later gave some of her *Sprites* to Wright. He used them mostly as garden ornaments in the courtyards at Taliesin and in the gardens at Taliesin West. A replica today stands sentinel at the back entrance to Wright's Oak Park home and studio in the shade of a mature ginkgo tree.

In the 1980s, replicas of Wright's *Sprites* – approximately six feet tall and weighing 450lbs (over 200g/32stone) – were installed in the Arizona Biltmore Resort & Spa in Phoenix where they can still be seen. The Frank Lloyd Wright Foundation has also authorized reproduction of the *Sprites* for sale to the public as garden ornaments.

Two other Wright sculptures that have been reproduced as garden or courtyard accents are the female and male Native Americans *Nokoma* and *Nakomis*. *Nakoma* is pleasantly rounded in form, seen with a bowed head, carrying a bowl and a papoose on her back. Inset at her side is her daughter, carrying a smaller bowl. The Native American warrior in much more angular form, wears a feathered headdress. His head bent forward, he is showing his son how to use a bow and arrow. The 18-foot tall *Nakomis* and 12-foot tall *Nakoma* today decorate a courtyard at the Johnson Administration Building, Racine, Wisconsin, which Wright designed. In the 1950s, a Taliesin apprentice, Giovanni del Drago, replicated the sculptures in plaster, and these now feature in the garden at the Hillside School building, Taliesin.

After completing Midway Gardens, Wright decided that it was too stressful working with other sculptors in the creation of his ideas, and never again worked in collaboration. However, he encouraged his apprentices to express themselves in sculpture, and some of their work decorates Taliesin West. One such sculptor, Heloise Crista, joined the Fellowship, not to become an architect but to broaden her skills as an artist. She said: "Frank Lloyd Wright was about more than architecture. The principles used in organic architecture of which he spoke are in a broad sense applicable to all creative work, all artistic work in general." Crista lives in what was once an apprentice apartment and sells her sculpture, which Wright greatly admired. Wright invited her to make a bronze bust of him,

Solar Wind, a sculpture by Heloise Crista on a terrace at Taliesin West.

101

and though a number were made of Wright during his lifetime, he declared Crista's his favourite. Castings of her original design are displayed on tables at Taliesin, in the living room, and Taliesin West, in the garden room.

The abstraction of trees and flowers is a favourite motif in many of Wright's screen and window decorations. For the Darwin D. Martin House, in Buffalo, New York, the stained glass design for a window is known as the *Tree of Life*. It shows three straight stylized tree trunks rising from stylized pots to create an abstract foliage canopy. Another image, designed as a magazine cover, is entitled *Saguaro Forms & Cactus Flowers*. Reminiscent of desert Indian blanket designs and using the colours of desert flowers, the design now forms a backlit glass mural at the Arizona Biltmore, Phoenix.

For the Dana House, in Springfield, Illinois, Wright designed 450 pieces of art in glass and 103 items of furniture. One of these glass pieces, entitled *Sumac Screen*, shows an abstraction of sumac, a hardy native tree that Wright admired for its dramatic fall foliage. Spires of corn, sunbursts of water lily petals, and other plants surrounding

Taliesin and Taliesin West, became abstractions of Wright's window, wall and screen designs.

In his Oak Park house and studio, and in other residences he designed, Wright liked to set stained glass art abstractions into first floor windows to screen the interior from passers-by since he disliked the use of curtains or drapes. A particularly beautiful skylight at the Oak Park home contains an abstraction of tree foliage. Where privacy was not such a problem, he created many windows with clear glass, but designed them and placed them in such a way that they provided an interesting view or created an interesting shape. Wide banks of windows at Taliesin, for example, take in panoramic views, while individual windows frame specific views.

During the construction of Tokyo's Imperial Hotel, Wright had spent time in Shanghai, supervising carpet designs woven by Chinese rug makers, and had bought many Chinese artworks. Much of Wright's personal collection of oriental art was lost in a fire that swept Taliesin after a thunderstorm sparked a fire in 1924. However, two significant examples of Chinese art are used as garden ornament at

A pair of *Fu Dogs* (also called lions) stand on pedestals in the lower courtyard at Taliesin.

A sculpture by Carl Milles entitled *Pioneer Wife* at Taliesin rises from an oriental urn at the entrance to Wright's living quarters.

Taliesin on the escarpment wall facing the Wisconsin River and Spring Green. Known as *Fu Dogs* (also called lions), they are displayed at opposite ends of the wall in the lower entry court. Fu dogs traditionally guard Chinese temples to ward off evil spirits. Made of bronze, they stand five feet high, and Wisconsin's harsh winter climate threatened to destroy them. However, a conservation effort recently restored them like new, and a coat of wax was added for protection against the climate.

A Carl Milles bronze sculpture, *Jonah and the Whale*, is used as a fountain ornament for one of the courtyard pools. Another Milles piece, *Pioneer Wife*, showing a woman with a rooster in her arms, rises from a bronze bowl at the entrance to the living quarters. "I'm crazy about her," wrote Wright in a thank-you to his sculptor friend.

A beautiful blue ceramic Chinese urn occupies a stone pedestal between two flights of steps leading from the lower court to the entrance to the living quarters. Since the steps are permanently shaded by tall trees and the house foundation walls, the vessel makes a striking focal point.

A dominant feature of the Hill Garden at Taliesin is a turquoise bowl called a Souchow tub. A smaller open container at the entrance to Wright's drafting studio, echoes the shape of the Souchow tub. These are not intended for planting, since the dark hole signifies the allure of black holes in nature, for example hollow trees and caves. A pair of oriental kettles, with lids in the shape of lotus leaves, adds an oriental flavour to one of the courtyards.

For many years a large cast iron Chinese temple bell hung from a branch of a bur oak that shaded the Tea Circle. But after the oak blew down in a storm in 1998, the bell was positioned on an entry wall to the Hill Garden. "Its resonance – thirty-two seconds – is remarkable," according to Frances Nemtin.

Numerous planters are used for decorative effect at Wright's Oak Park home and studio, also at Taliesin and Taliesin West. A particular dish planter used at the entrance to Wright's studio features a rounded bowl and square base, signifying Wright's logo at the time. Over the years he changed his logo to a red square with a square spiral, and then a red square with squared labyrinth design.

ABOVE: An ornamental oriental urn, decorates a flight of steps leading from the lower courtyard to the upper courtyard at Taliesin.

FAR LEFT: A Chinese kettle with a lotus decoration above the plunge pool at Taliesin.

LEFT: During his career Wright created and used several logos. This labyrinth design decorates the entrance to Taliesin West.

A prairie garden almost entirely of purple coneflowers (*Echinacea purpurea*) at Taliesin.

6 The influence of JENS JENSEN

The distinguished landscape gardener Jens Jensen (1860–1951) became a close friend of Frank Lloyd Wright when Wright lived at Oak Park, and Jensen was establishing himself in Chicago as a landscape designer after working for the Chicago Parks Department. Jensen disliked the term "landscape architect" and preferred to be called a landscaper. He believed that landscaping and architecture were contradictions – the one seeking to preserve green space and the other often the means to destroy or spoil it. In spite of that view, he was a great admirer of Wright's work and applauded Wright's efforts to make his buildings blend in with their surroundings. Cornelia Brierly remembers Jensen fondly: "He came to Taliesin often. We used to take nature walks together. He was a wonderful person."

Speaking of Frank Lloyd Wright, Jensen wrote in his book *Siftings* (Johns Hopkins University Press): "Perhaps no section of America has so far shown as much power in the development of native art as the prairie country. Here lived and worked the great architect whose forms were inspired by the horizontal lines of the plains and whose decorative art grew out of his love for the native prairie thistle, a plant full of poetry and beauty."

He and Wright shared similar views about preparing students for careers in their respective professions. At Taliesin, Wright demanded that his students work in his orchards and vegetable plots, growing their own food and cultivating flowers for cutting. In this way, he believed, they would develop a special respect for nature and not only take inspiration from it, but also seek to preserve it. At Taliesin West he required his students to spend nights in the desert, camping, in order for them to get to know the desert's sculptural forms, its sounds and pristine tranquillity – again to underscore the power of the desert to inspire architectural innovation and instil a passion for conservation. And at Taliesin, even today, the students maintain a large productive organic vegetable

Landscape architect Jens Jensen beside a saguaro cactus at Taliesin West.

garden, care for an orchard and vineyard, and maintain a large triangular-shaped rhubarb patch at a turn in the road connecting Midway Farm, Hillside and Taliesin.

Robert E. Grese, author of the biography, *Jens Jensen: Maker of Natural Parks and Gardens* (Johns Hopkins University Press), reveals Jensen's methods for teaching students landscape design to be similar to Wright's: "As a model for designers, Jensen's approach stressed the clear need for careful study of natural landscapes. He objected to design training that was purely academic. He felt that an intimate knowledge of plants and horticulture and a genuine sense of humility were essential for landscape design to reach the level of art. In his case, this meant a lifetime of studying forests, prairies, wetlands, patterns of sunlight, soils, and rock formations, as well as an understanding of human behaviour and cultural traditions."

Jensen advised his landscaping students, "First grow cabbages. After that plant a flower. When you have successfully grown a flower, then you can start to think about growing a tree. After watching a tree grow for several years, observing how its character develops from year to year, then you can think of a composition of living plants – a composition of life itself. Then you will know what landscape architecture is."

Jensen was the leading advocate of the "Prairie Style" of landscaping, which Wright endorsed. In Wright's essay, "Chicago Culture," Wright wrote of Jensen: "Chicago has a native nature poet who has made the West Park system a delight to the country. He is a true interpreter of the peculiar charm of our prairie landscape."

Thistledown in midsummer borders the water garden at Taliesin. Both Jensen and Wright loved the native prairie thistle for its architectural beauty.

For Jensen the prairie had an abundance of indigenous flowers and organic forms found nowhere else on earth, and he felt little need to import plants of foreign origin for its gardens. Recalling his first garden design for the Chicago parks department, Jensen wrote: "I had a great collection of perennial wildflowers. We couldn't get the stock from nurserymen, as there had never been requests for it, and we went out into the woods with a team and a wagon, and carted it in ourselves. Each plant was given room to grow as it wanted to. People enjoyed seeing the garden. They exclaimed excitedly when they saw flowers they recognized; they welcomed them as they would a friend from home. This was the first natural garden in Chicago . . . To my delight the transplantings flourished and after a while I did away with formal beds."

Wright's analysis of Jensen as a "native nature poet" is apt. Speaking about his work, Jensen wrote: "To me the art of landscaping is more closely associated with music than any other art. Its rhythm and its tonal qualities are as a folk song or a sonata. For a friend I planted a group of sumac on a hillock facing the setting sun. When autumn's frosty breath turned their leafy crowns into a flaming red, my friend called it the "Tannhauser Group."

The "friend" referred to in this paragraph is believed to be Frank Lloyd Wright, since Wright loved listening to Wagner's *Tannhauser* overture, and a clump of sumac still crowns a hill at Taliesin and also the roadside verges leading to the property. Jensen visited Taliesin and also Taliesin West and advised Wright on landscaping both properties. Indeed, Jensen even went to the trouble of purchasing for Wright plants he felt should be used at Taliesin, on one occasion ordering a large shipment of bare-root native perennials and shrubs from a Rochester, New York, mail order nursery. The package, addressed to "Frank Lloyd Wright, of Spring Green, Wisconsin," contained prairie plants such as summer phlox, beebalm, black-eyed Susans, purple coneflowers, scarlet honeysuckle and Kansas gayfeather, all seen at Taliesin today.

Jensen was a striking figure, with a memorable presence. A picture of health and vitality during his landscaping years, he was six feet tall with bright blue eyes, a bushy moustache that could hide a family of sparrows, and matching eyebrows. His vigorous red hair turned white in his later years, but he always maintained a pencil-straight military bearing. He spoke with a heavy Danish accent in a voice that exuded enthusiasm and strong opinions. Born near Dybbol, Denmark to a prosperous farming family, he grew up on his family's farm.

"This understanding of the immediate environment, this knowledge of the mysteries of the sea and the land across the fjord, and those stories of the Vikings of an earlier period who dared the sea and the unknown for adventure, stimulated the imagination and left their unmistakable mark on the growing mind," wrote Jensen in 1939. His upbringing was similar to Wright's, and in his book *Siftings*, he echoes Wright's love of nature in words similar to those of Wright's *Autobiography* when Wright felt uplifted by the early spring appearance of pasque flowers on his uncle's farm. Jensen wrote: "When the first flowers appeared in spring, father made pilgrimages with his boys to the bluffs towering above the open sea. Can anyone realize what it meant to those who had been shut in for months to be greeted again by the warmth-bringing rays of the sun and the lovely green it brought forth, changing the earth into a new beauty?"

Jensen emigrated to the United States in 1884, aged 24. In Denmark he had studied agriculture and in the US worked as a labourer, eventually for the West Parks Commission in Chicago where, in spite of no formal training as a landscape architect, he gained experience as a landscaper and architect. In particular he formulated innovative design ideas that sought to preserve a feeling of the prairie that then surrounded Chicago. Jensen's architectural work included garden and park structures, such as stone meeting circles, naturalistic rock-rimmed swimming pools and glass conservatories. His conservationist spirit so pleased the Parks Department that Jensen was promoted to superintendent and then, in 1909, he struck out on his own as an independent landscaper and consultant. Over the course of his career he created Columbus Park on the western side of Chicago, and redesigned Humboldt, Garfield and Douglas Parks, in addition to fifteen smaller ones, parks for other cities, plus

Jensen and Wright shared an appreciation for the native sumac, and the hillside planting of a group at Taliesin may have been done by Jensen. Wright so much admired the palm-like leaf clusters that he incorporated abstract designs of them into glasswork.

RIGHT: A border planting of prairie wildflowers near Taliesin, featuring purple coneflowers, beebalm (*Monarda*) and black-eyed Susans (*Rudbeckia hirta*).

BELOW: Pasque flowers (*Pulsatilla vulgaris*) are among the earliest to bloom at Taliesin.

dozens of private properties, including those of the clients of Frank Lloyd Wright. In a letter dated April 2, 1923, from Wright to Louis H. Sullivan (his mentor, former employer and client, with whom he was now reconciled) Wright wrote: "A nice note from Jens. What a loveable soul he is . . ."

Wright's landscape design concepts and Jensen's were similar, both preferring an emphasis on indigenous plants in the creation of naturalistic – rather than formal – landscapes. Jensen landscaped Wright's Coonley House and Booth House

projects, and he worked on Wright's Midway Gardens.

In particular, Jensen echoed Wright's liking for native trees to frame his houses. When Wright met the British architect, Sir Clough Williams-Ellis during a visit to his country estate near Portmeirion, in Wales, Wright remarked how the old Welsh oaks surrounding the property gave it great character. Jensen, in his book *Siftings*, writes extensively about the allure of native trees to landscape Mid-Western properties. Commenting on the white birch, or canoe birch, he declared: "The canoe birch is really the poet of our northern woods. A pure stand of birch trees is quite a revelation . . . The reflected light of moonbeams playing on the white bark of the birches illuminates the woodlands with a surprising clearness." A cluster of canoe birch greets visitors to the entrance to Wright's Taliesin residence.

Jensen sang the praises of many other native woody plants, including the dogwood, redbud, shadblow, cottonwood, aspen, prairie crab-apple, hawthorn, locust, juniper, sumac, and white oak. All are part of the landscape surrounding Taliesin.

The Tea Circle, crowning the cluster of courtyards at Taliesin, is similar to Jensen's signature "council rings" or "meeting circles", which feature a fire pit in the middle. In *Siftings*, describing a commission that particularly pleased him, Jensen explains his liking for the stone circles: "Just below the slope of the ravine the first council ring was built — a new adventure. In this friendly circle around the fire, man becomes himself. Here there is no social caste. All are on the same level, looking each other in the face. A ring speaks of strength and friendship and is one of the great symbols of mankind. The fire in the centre portrays the beginning of civilization, and it is around the fire our forefathers gathered when they first placed foot on this continent . . . The smoke of the fire illuminated by the moon, forms fantastic shapes, which float gently over the deep and penetrating shadows of the ravine. Many of these rings I have built since this first attempt. When they are placed on school grounds or in playfields, I call them story rings. These rings are the beginning of a new social life in the gardens of the America of tomorrow."

The allure of a fire both inside and outside the house, appealed to Wright. During his lifetime Wright designed more than two thousand fireplaces, no two the same. He designed thirty-four for his three homes, usually using brick or natural stone. He considered the fireplace the heart of a home, and the hearth a gathering place for the family to sit around and bond. When the human species first evolved on earth, the family unit gathered around a fire for warmth and safety, and the flickering flames stimulate creative thought. Wright noted that when Indian tribal leaders needed to meet and discuss tribal policy they did so around a fire, often in the open. Wright's Tea Circle at Taliesin was a favourite place for Wright and his apprentices to gather in the mid-afternoon. Like Jensen's meeting circles, the centre featured a fire pit (now used as a small garden bed).

Jensen's landscape style and particular enthusiasms can be seen reflected in many of Wright's gardens. Jensen started a design by inspecting the site for distinctive natural features and designed around them. He was particularly fond of natural woodland, streams, water views, ravines, hillocks and meadows. Usually he would introduce a grove of long-lived native deciduous trees, such as bur oaks for their majesty and sugar maples for their intense autumn colours. Around the edges, or as an under-storey, he would

partner these with smaller woody plants such as the prairie crab-apple for its cloud of pink flowers, to create "poetic compositions." He liked to make the driveway a visual adventure, to install a naturalistic water feature using native stone (usually overlapping flat flagstone to simulate the horizontal strata of prairie outcrops). Woodland usually featured a carpet of shade-loving wildflowers such as cheerful blue wood violets, shimmering white trillium and floriferous yellow lady's-slipper orchids among native ferns. Invariably the woodland would feature a clearing with a meeting circle and fire pit, while meadows used native grasses in great sweeps, the edges and islands within the grass planted with drifts of prairie wildflowers, such as purple coneflower, yellow black-eyed Susans, pink liatris and pink and red shades of summer phlox.

Jensen loved curves in a landscape. "The study of curves is the study of life itself," he said. "Curves represent the unchained mind full of mystery and beauty . . . Landscaping must follow the lines of the free-flowing tree with its thousands of curves."

Of a water feature he installed, Jensen wrote: "On the hillside, not seen from the house, we built a swimming hole. It was hewn out of the hillside and reached by intimate

Native paper birch (*Betula papyrifera*) was one of Wright's and Jensen's favourite trees for the way its gleaming white bark shows up in woodland.

115

A small Jensen-style meeting circle at Kentuck Knob, Pennsylvania.

A Jensen-style meeting circle in the Sonoran Desert at Taliesin West.

trails. On moonlight nights this pool holds a spell over all who visit it. Can you envision moonbeams and deep shadows reflected in the water, or the soft light of the moon lighting up gay flowers planted in the crevices . . . With a bit of imagination one can see the dance of the wood nymphs."

Inspiration for these naturalistic swimming holes came from the high bluffs of stratified rock along the Illinois, Rock and Mississippi Rivers. Jensen edged streams and ponds with similar stratified rock ledges.

When Wright decided to start his school for architects at Taliesin, he wanted Jens to be listed among the Fellowships' supporters and occasional lecturers. On December 28, 1928,

Wright wrote to Jensen, seeking his support: "Now I believe the creative instinct in Man is that quality of faculty in him of getting himself reborn and born again . . . And that Jens, is why I am interested in this proposed school. I should like you to be one to initiate steps that would put a little experimental station at work where this thing might be wooed and won, if only to a small extent."

Jensen was seventy-five when he received this invitation to be among "The Friends of the Taliesin Fellowship" and he already had planned to create his own school of learning in Wisconsin. This may be why he elected not to accept Wright's invitation. Nevertheless, Jensen continued to visit

Taliesin. In a December 20 1934 local newspaper column, Cornelia Brierly reported that Wright and Jensen had just met at Taliesin. Calling Jens Jensen, "The poet naturalist", she stated: "With different words these two strong men sing a freedom song for the beauty of America." And in a letter to Wright on January 30, 1935, Jensen wrote of this Taliesin visit: "I can still see, in the fading light of a late December day, Taliesin peacefully coming out of the ancient cliffs of which it is a part."

Later that year Jensen moved from Chicago to a property he had used as a summer retreat in northern Wisconsin, and established "The Clearing", a school to teach his landscaping and conservation philosophies. Wright himself lectured at The Clearing. During his younger years Jensen had lobbied for the creation of the Cook County Forest Preserve District, the Illinois state park system, the Indiana Dunes Park, the National Lakeshore and The Friends of Our Native Landscape, for which Wright designed the letterhead as a gift to his friend. At every opportunity Jensen advocated means for people to have greater contact with nature, particularly indigenous colonies of flowers and plants. Harold Henderson, writing in 1985 about Jensen, said: "He was a reformer with his hands on a spade and his head in the clouds."

Another Jensen-influenced meeting circle, this time at Taliesin. The small square flower bed in the centre was originally a fire pit.

A majestic bur oak (*Quercus macrocarpa*), a native tree much used and respected by both Jensen and Wright, in the landscape below Taliesin.

7 Other Wright LANDSCAPES

To understand Wright's landscape philosophy more fully, I have chosen to focus on several important commissions beyond those located near his Oak Park home and studio (see pages 22–37). They are Kentuck Knob, representing perhaps the best example of Wright's Usonian residential designs; Monona Terrace, Madison, a municipal building he designed with an ambitious roof garden; the Robie House, an example of his prairie style houses where lack of space around the house necessitated the introduction of plantings through built-in containers; and The Walker House, Carmel, California, a coastal garden where wind and salt spray present daunting landscape difficulties.

Kentuck Knob, Pennsylvania

Wright built Kentuck Knob in 1954 for the Hagan family, owners of the Hagan Ice Cream Company. It is now owned by the British art collector and architecture connoisseur Peter, Lord Palumbo. The hilly 79-acre property is located just seven miles from Fallingwater in Pennsylvania's Laurel Highlands at 2,000 feet above sea level. Wright made no prior site inspection, content to design the house from studying black and white photographs and a map showing topographical features. When Wright received the commission, the site was completely bare of vegetation as a result of poor, chalky soil and its exposure to winds. Although this absence of trees provided sweeping panoramic views, Mr. And Mrs. I. N. Hagan planted thousands of native trees for shelter. Wright always advocated the use of indigenous trees to improve a site, and the Hagans followed this landscaping edict. They planted 8,800 seedling trees and mostly selected species for their brilliant autumn leaf colour. A sample invoice from Mrs Hagan's main supplier, Musser Forest Nursery, shows the purchase of 1,000 tulip poplar, 1000 white ash, 1,500 sugar maple, 1,000 Canadian hemlock, 500 white oak, 500 shellbark hickory and 500 pin oak.

Kentuck Knob nestles below the brow of a hill 2,000 feet above sea level, once bare of vegetation. The original owners followed Wright's injunction to plant only indigenous trees.

> **"** *Wright said a house should be a noble consort between man and the trees, and that is what Kentuck became.* **"**

DONALD HOFFMAN *Frank Lloyd Wright's House on Kentuck Knob* UNIVERSITY OF PITTSBURG PRESS

Other purchases included hundreds of native American dogwood, mostly white. Tolerant of shade, these were used to line the driveway, though many have since died. "In the spring these dogwood trees were like white clouds," wrote Mrs Hagan in her memoir of Kentuck Knob.

Today the site is surrounded by woodland, with gaps in the trees to provide views into the surrounding countryside. A steep, narrow driveway meanders in from the main road to a spacious courtyard and a U-shaped residence immediately identifiable as a Wright masterpiece. The single-storey house wraps around a hexagonal gravel courtyard that draws inspiration from traditional Japanese house designs; there are large picture windows, and a low pitch to the roof. In a Japanese-garden-like setting of boulders, ferns and evergreen groundcover, tall evergreens and deciduous trees produce a feeling of tranquillity, veiling Wright's sharp geometric lines,.

In spite of his clean, modernistic designs, Wright had a keen sensitivity to the natural environment and deliberately sought dramatic contrasts of rectilinear geometric shapes and the rounded, flowing lines of nature. He decreed that "houses should not be built on top of hills, but *of* them so hill and house are integrated . . . each the happier for the other." And so Kentuck Knob rests snugly in the brow of the hill, like Taliesin, protruding into its leafy surroundings like a rock shelf.

The driveway of almost a half mile sweeps uphill in a gracious curve so the house with its dramatic stone terraces

OPPOSITE: A pyramid of boulders by British sculptor, Andy Goldsworthy, fits perfectly into its woodland setting.

ABOVE: Three British telephone kiosks are part of Lord Palumbo's sculpture collection at Kentuck Knob.

is revealed at the last moment in its cathedral of trees, as if it is an extension of the hill. The masonry prow of the main terrace surges 18 feet into the air, like a ship cresting a wave. Around the house are woodland trails.

Reminiscent of Japanese Imperial gardens, a path of rough flagstone stepping stones, leads from the patio across a lightly shaded lawn to a spectacular panoramic view, from where gravel trails lead downhill to the Sculpture Meadow, where visitors today can view Lord Palumbo's eclectic outdoor sculpture collection, including two substantial pieces by British sculptor Andy Goldsworthy. The inclusion of Goldsworthy's work is appropriate, for Goldsworthy creates organic sculpture, using elements taken directly from nature, like rough fieldstone, leaf stems and even icicles, like those elements that Wright worked into some of his window and door designs. A pyramid composed of large rounded boulders rises below the house in woodland, next to a circular enclosure made of local stone reminiscent of sheep shelters on the Yorkshire Moors. Close by Goldsworthy's circular farm wall is a rectangular upright section of graffiti-covered Berlin Wall. Three red British telephone kiosks stand sentry along a ridge, a whimsical apple core sculpture rests in an old orchard, and an entire field of red metal silhouettes representing "The Red Army", dazzles the eye. Except for the addition of the sculpture collection, the property remains faithful to the period when the Hagans lived there.

Monona Terrace, Wisconsin

One of Wright's most controversial designs was Monona Terrace, a community and convention centre for downtown Madison, Wisconsin. Although he designed the structure in 1938 as a "dream civic centre", the project became stalled in political squabbles for more than fifty years. Wright's vision for a link between the City and Lake Monona was finally realized in 1997. Viewed from the middle of the lake, the modernistic low-profile building has massive arched windows that curve out over the lake, and a large roof garden in perfect alignment with the Greek revival State Capitol

Building behind. Wright designed the impressive rooftop garden – known as the William T. Evjue Rooftop Garden (for its donor) – with raised planters for trees and shrubs, and spaces for combinations of annuals and perennials.

The Robie House, Chicago

Now owned by the University of Chicago, the Robie House is located close to Jens Jensen's "meeting circles" at Promontory Point, on Lakeshore Drive. It is considered the finest example of Wright's prairie style architecture. Long, sleek balconies occupy a small urban lot with little room for gardens or even foundation plantings. To compensate for a lack of vegetation, Wright's original design features long terrace planters and Wright-designed dish planters that seem to be inspired by Mayan architecture (see pages 30–32). However, owing to the cost of maintaining such an expanse of container planting, only several small sections of the balcony planters are filled today.

Walker House, California

This Usonian–style coastal vacation cottage is built on a rocky promontory overlooking Monterey Bay at Carmel. Mature cypress trees shelter the rear of the property and veil the living quarters from the highway, but because of exposure to wind and salt spray, substantial plantings are difficult to maintain. A wooden, batten privacy fence along the property line, facing the coastal road, shelters a strip of perennials planted between boulders, and one of the entrance pillars features a Wright dish planter. The roadside plantings include purple-flowering sea statice (*Limonium* species) and Mediterranean rock roses (*Cistus* species) in pink and white. Otherwise the predominant flowering plant for the sunlit areas is the native California ice plant. Used as a ground cover, its succulent leaves and yellow or pink flowers creep over the bare rocks and cascade like a curtain towards the sandy shoreline. It is highly salt and wind tolerant and is resistant to low rainfall.

After Wright's involvement in the construction and landscaping of what he called The Cabin, some plants did

OPPOSITE: The roof garden at Wright's Monona Terrace, Madison, Wisconsin. A bed of native black-eyed Susans and purple coneflowers contrast with a bed of non-native feather reed grass (*Calamagrostis* x *acutiflora* 'Karl Foerster') and Russian sage (*Perovskia atriplicifolia*).

not thrive, and Mrs. Walker consulted California landscape architect Thomas Church. When Wright heard this he shot off a letter chiding her for employing a professional landscaper ". . . to undo all I have done. If you did employ one," he said, "It is the first time it has happened to me in a long lifetime of building." He concluded: "I hope what I hear is not true and love's labour not lost. I love the Cabin and had it in my heart as well as my head."

Mrs. Walker replied: "What a scolding!! And I don't deserve it. Nothing has been done to harm *our* house . . . I asked Tommy Church, whom I have known since I was a child, to help me . . . I planted myself about 2,000 succulents or ice plants and brought rocks from the beach . . . to put in places where you said they should go . . ." She explained that the only change she made as a result of consulting with Church was putting gravel where Wright had wanted grass because grass was proving difficult to maintain. "But if you do not like it, out it comes," she insisted. "No real change has been made . . . His one idea has been to follow the little sketches in planting that you made."

RIGHT: The Robie House, Chicago, showing window box planters filled with sweet potato vines (*Ipomoea batatas*) to drape down from the terraces like a curtain. Wright's original plan was for the curtains of foliage to extend the entire length of every terrace, but today cost of maintenance has reduced the container plantings to a token display.

OVERLEAF: Wright's Carmel Cottage (also known as the Walker House), at Carmel California, shows the triangular terrace extending out from a grove of native Monterey cypress into Monterey Bay like the prow of a ship.

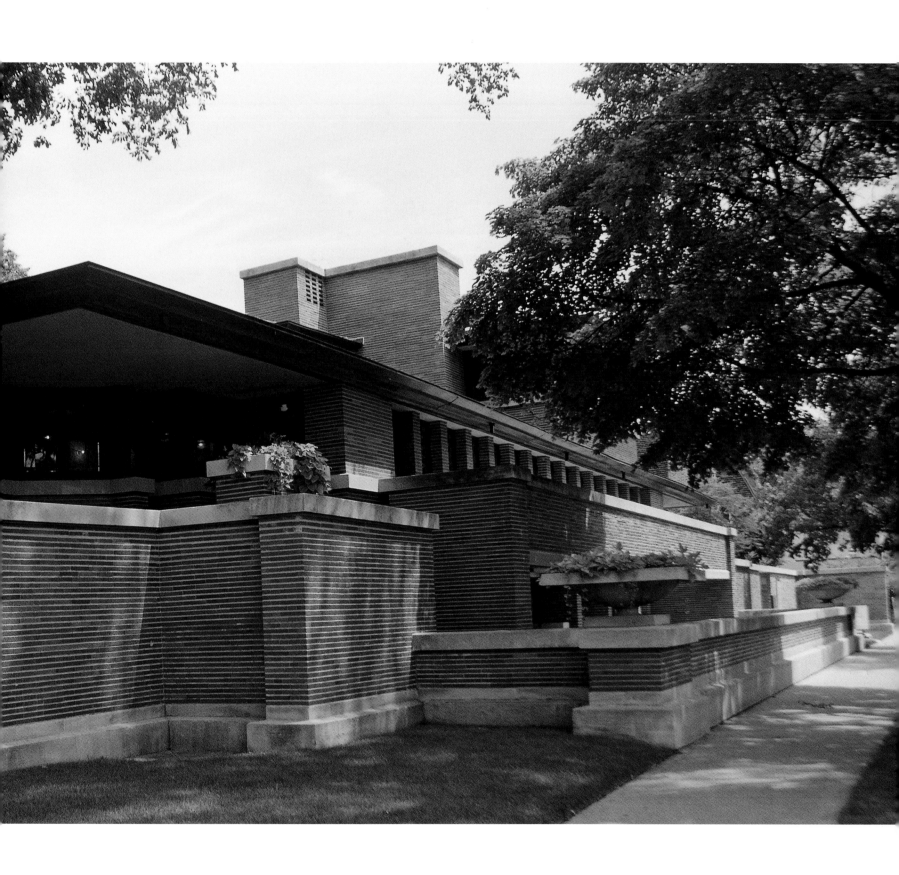

"A light blanket of snow fresh-fallen over sloping fields, gleaming in the morning sun. Clusters of pod-topped weeds woven of bronze here and there sprinkling the spotless expanse of white. Dark sprays of slender metallic straight lines, tipped with quivering dots. Pattern to the eye of the sun, as the sun spreads a delicate network of more pattern in blue shadows on the white beneath."

FRANK LLOYD WRIGHT'S AUTOBIOGRAPHY

8 WRIGHT'S PRAIRIE STYLE GARDEN

The above quotation describes a section of prairie meadow adjacent to a relative's farm in Wisconsin that Wright eventually purchased to create Taliesin. This observation by Wright shows his acute sensitivity to nature. His ability to integrate architecture into nature's ephemeral beauty was key to his success as an architect.

When Wright first established Taliesin, on the brow of a hill, the surrounding hills were more open, like true prairie grasslands, than they are today. In early spring they bloomed with blue birdsfoot violets and purple and white pasque flowers (*Pulsatilla vulgaris*) that cloaked the ground with silky seed tassels after the purple anemone-like flowers are faded.

Later in the season, about mid-July, the prairie is a sea of even more vibrant colour, from drifts of purple coneflowers, yellow black-eyed Susans, pink bergamot and a host of other hardy perennials. Wright liked to bring the prairie wildflowers into his cultivated garden, using them in mixed perennial borders, and today a large expanse of prairie garden still survives below the Romeo and Juliet windmill he built at the crest of a hill. The prairie hillside was planted by ploughing the ground and seeding. The principle components of this planting are drought tolerant. Locally, on areas of grassland prairie between woodland and cultivated fields, stretches of prairie are still spangled with wildflowers, either planted by nature or planted by property owners to maintain the prairie look.

What makes a prairie garden different from a meadow garden is the choice of plants. Although many of the influential Dutch landscape designer Piet Oudolf's naturalistic gardens have been described as prairie gardens, a true prairie garden must contain only plants indigenous to the North American prairie. Most prairie gardens installed by European designers contain plants native to Europe or Asia as well as North America, such as European feather reed

Ornamental grasses persist well into winter and look attractive covered in snow.

133

OPPOSITE: Wright's Romeo
and Juliet windmill at
Taliesin rises above a prairie
hillside spangled with yellow
(drooping) coneflower
(*Ratibida pinnata*).

Beebalm

islands of bare soil within the grassy area, and seed these bare patches. Be sure to avoid hybrids, since hybrid varieties are generally sterile and will not reseed.

A misconception about prairie gardens is that they are all the same height, sheered by the wind, and usually topping off at four feet. In fact many prairie plantings in nature feature tall growing species, up to seven feet and it is the tall towering plants that Wright liked to see, striking the sky like minarets or exclamation points in the landscape. Some of these tall varieties include dusky pink Joe-pye weed, magenta ironweed, white Virginia spires, and yellow prairie dock.

Following are some of the most prolific prairie wildflowers surrounding Taliesin today at the height of summer. All relish a sunny location.

Black-eyed Susan

Beebalm, wild bergamot (*Monarda fistulosa*)

Although there are many different colours of beebalm, including white, red and purple, the most prolific prairie beebalm is pink. Plants grow to 3ft/90cm high, have a spicy fragrance resembling the aroma of Earl Grey tea, which is flavoured with bergamot, an asian citrus fruit. Beebalm tolerates drought and poor soil. The flowers are tubular, arranged in a crown, and they are highly attractive to both hummingbirds and butterflies. Zones 4–9.

Black-eyed Susan (*Rudbeckia hirta*)

The golden yellow daisy-like flowers have black seed centres and measure up to 3in/7.6cm across. They grow to 3ft/90cm high, tolerate poor soil and drought. They are good companions to purple coneflowers, flowering at the same time. Seed of both kinds is relished by songbirds such as goldfinches that will alight on the domed heads and peck away at the ripe seed, much of which spills to the ground around the plant. Zones 4–9.

Cup plant (*Silphium perfoliatum*)

Plants generally grow to 7ft/2m high, the strong, erect stems topped by 34in/710cm wide yellow daisy-like flowers, resembling a sunflower. Zones 4–9.

Cup plant

grass, misty blue Siberian sage and yellow Mediterranean verbascum.

To establish a prairie garden, select a prairie mixture from a mail order wildflower source, till the ground so there is bare soil and sprinkle the seed at the rate recommended on the bag either in early spring, even before the last frosts, or in early autumn. Prairie gardens can also be planted from transplants purchased from local garden centres, but that is a much more expensive proposition than growing from seed.

If you have a large meadow, another idea is to create

Gayfeather

Culver's root (*Veronicastrum virginicum*)

These tall, sturdy plants grow to 6ft/1.8m high, topped by sharp-looking spires of white or pale pink flower clusters. Avoid hybrids which will not self-seed. Zones 3–9.

Gayfeather (*Liatris* species)

Most are stiff, spire-like plants growing in clumps to 3ft/90cm high. Some flower from the top down; others from the bottom up. The pink bristle-like flowers make a good contrast to prairie grasses. *L. spicata* blooms from the top of the plant to the bottom and is the most desirable for a prairie planting, growing to 4ft/1.2m high. *L. pychnostachys* blooms from the bottom to the top. Zones 3–9.

ABOVE: Ironweed

LEFT: Indian blanket

Indian blanket (*Gaillardia pulchella*)

This has red daisy-like flowers up to 3in/7.6cm wide, each petal tipped yellow. Plants grow to 2ft/60cm, with slender, smooth leaves. Blooming in early summer, if the spent flowers are picked blooming will continue into autumn. Grown as an annual, this species is suitable for all zones. A related perennial species, *G. aristata*, has mostly yellow petals, with a red zone at the base. Zones 3–8.

Ironweed, giant ironweed (*Vernonia crinita*)

A tall grower like Joe-Pye weed (up to 6ft/1.8m), the purple flowers resemble thistles and are held in erect clusters. They attract butterflies and though they are drought resistant, the most vigorous plantings are in moist soil. A good companion to black-eyed Susans over which it towers. Zones 5–7.

Joe-Pye weed (*Eupatorium maculatum*)

The tallest growing of prairie flowers and it is naturalized over many parts of Europe in addition to wet meadows of its native North America. Plants grow to 6ft/1.8m high, topped by billowing clusters of fluffy dusky-pink flowers up to 10in/25cm across. Although it is drought resistant, the biggest flowers and most vigorous plantings occur in moist soils. Zones 3–9.

Lance-leaved coreopsis (*Coreopsis lanceolata*)

Daisy-like yellowflowers up to 2in/5cm wide resemble small sunflowers. Growing on 2ft/60cm plants, with slender, grass-like leaves, plants bloom from mid-summer until frosts. A related species, *C. tinctoria*, is annual, growing to four feet high. The flowers are slightly smaller, and come in a variety of colours, mostly yellow, maroon, and yellow with a red zone at the petal base. Zones 3–9.

Milkweed (*Asclepias* species)

The two best species for prairie gardens are the orange-flowered butterfly weed (*A. tuberosa*) and the pink milkweed (*A. incarnata*). Butterfly weed has clusters of small star-shaped flowers that attract hordes of butterflies.

Joe-Pye weed

Lance-leaved coreopsis

Purple coneflower

Butterfly milkweed

Summer phlox

Yellow or drooping coneflower

It grows to 2ft/60cm high. Pink milkweed grows taller, up to 3ft/90cm, has its star-shaped flowers arranged is a larger cluster (up to 6in/15cm) across, and reaches peak bloom a little later, although their flowering overlaps. Zones 3–9.

Purple coneflower (*Echinacea purpurea*)

Available mostly in purple, but also white, the daisy-like flowers can measure up to 4in/10cm across with a beautiful domed black seed cone in the centre. Plants grow to 3ft/60cm high, tolerate poor soil and drought. Clumps will double in size each year to create vast drifts. Zones 3–10.

Summer phlox (*Phlox paniculata*)

Though most wild species are subject to mildew, a fungus disease that coats the leaves with a powdery grey mould, this does not generally affect the flowering. Also, there are now mildew-resistant varieties available, such as the 'Volcano' series. Summer phlox produce bold, globular clusters of mostly red, pink, white and lavender flowers. They not only feature in prairie plantings but cultivated varieties are massed in the central courtyard facing Wright's bedroom, and also along the main perennial border overlooking the valley. They grow to 4ft/1.2m high, tolerate drought, but for the best floral display prefer a fertile soil. Zones 4–10.

Switchgrass (*Panicum virgatum*)

An vital component of the North American tall grass prairie, switchgrass grows erect straw-like stems that are mostly blue-green in summer, changing to orange in autumn. A bonus is the pink airy flower plume that glows when backlit. Generally growing 4ft/1.2m high, plants can grow taller in rich soil. It is decorative planted alone, as a small clump, or massed. Wright valued the dried orange stems and pink flower plumes for indoor arrangements. Zones 5–9.

Turk's-cap lily (*Lilium* species)

Prairie lilies were Wright's favourite flowers, and several species are indigenous to the US, including *L. pardalinum*, *L. superbum* and *L. michiganense*. They are all similar in appearance, producing orange flowers with recurved petals. Plants grow to 4ft/1.2m high. In the perennial beds of the Hill garden at Taliesin, a Japanese species (*L. lancifolium*), with larger flowers, is planted extensively. Commonly called tiger lily, it grows to 6ft/1.8m high. Mostly zones 4–7.

Yellow coneflower, drooping coneflower (*Ratibida pinnata*)

Similar in appearance to black-eyed Susans, the yellow coneflower has paler yellow petals that are swept back around a prominent black seed cone. A related species, Mexican hat (*R. columnifera*), has a taller black seed cone, raised high like a column, above maroon petals with yellow tips. Plants of both grow to 4ft/1.2m high, tolerate high heat, drought and poor soil. Zones 3–8.

Switch grass

Sedum 'Autumn Joy'

Turk's-cap lily

Black fountain grass

Fuller's teasel

Culver's root

There are many other native American wildflowers to be found around Taliesin in mid-summer, but the above varieties predominate. Many wayside plants are also evident, but most are not indigenous, including Queen Anne's lace, blue chicory from Europe, and the tawny daylily from Asia.

The plantings at Taliesin remain colourful into autumn when prairie asters and goldenrod bloom, and prairie grasses such as prairie dropseed, switchgrass and golden beard grass, turn amber shades. Many of these develop decorative seed heads that can look even more beautiful after a hoar frost coats their dried parts with ice.

At Taliesin today the perennial *Sedum* 'Autumn Joy' (syn. 'Herbstfreude') is used extensively in the cultivated gardens. Its flat flower clusters, red in late summer, turn to bronze as they dry and persist well after Christmas. Other favourites at Taliesin are the hardy shrub hydrangea 'Annabelle' whose white globular flowers dry to parchment brown. Alternating drifts of 'Autumn Joy' with clumps of 'Annabelle' and prairie grasses like switchgrass (*Panicum virgatum*) can create a beautiful border planting that looks especially lovely with light dustings of snow or hoar frost.

Other perennial plants some of which have been detailed above to consider for a beautiful dried effect in the landscape include:

Black fountain grass
(*Pennisetum alopecuroides* 'Moudry')

This striking plant forms a clump of slender arching leaf blades and smoky black seed heads on long straight stems. It is often preferred to pink fountain grass, which has light pink flowers, because black is a rare colour among dried plants. Zones 6–9.

Culver's root (*Veronicastrum virginicum*)

Dries to a cluster of dark brown minarets, similar to blue vervain (*Verbena hastata*). Both zones 3–9.

Siberian Iris

Globe Thistle

Yarrow 'Gold Plate'

Fuller's teasel (*Dipsacus fullonum*)

A biennial, whch readily naturalizes in moist meadows. It produces a cone-shaped seed head surrounded by pink flowers in summer, but dries naturally to a hard, spiny cone on strong dried stems by autumn. Zones 5–8.

Purple coneflower (*Echinacea purpurea*)

Develops a prominent seed disc that dries to black and looks stunning against the wispy silvery plumes of dried grasses. Zones 3–10.

Siberian iris (*Iris sibirica*)

Displays rigid brown stems topped by a poker like dark brown seed capsule. A massed planting of Siberian iris greets visitors to Wright's Oak Grove home and studio. Zones 4–9.

Thistle: Globe thistle (*Echinops ritro*) and sea holly (*Eryngium* species)

These ornamental thistles dry naturally to a papery texture. Globe thistle has ball-shaped spiny seed heads the size of a golf ball, while the sea hollies have a collar of spines surrounding a domed seed head. Zones 5 9.

Yarrow (*Achillea* species)

Comes in various colours, including yellow, pink, red and white, but it is the yellow, with flat flower umbels that creates the best dried seed heads. Zones 3–9.

Of course, all these die-hard varieties will look especially beautiful if planted with long-lasting berry-bearing bushes, like winterberry (*Ilex verticillata*) and firethorn (*Pyracantha coccinea*), also plants producing dramatic autumn foliage like blue stars (*Amsonia hubrechii*), that grows a billowing mass of slender orange leaves.

9 WRIGHT'S DESERT STYLE GARDEN

Wright's "desert style" of landscaping evolved from the challenge of living in an arid climate with such poor, stony soil that it could be dug only with a pickaxe. His desert style differs significantly from his prairie style of landscaping, not only because prairie plants are generally not suitable for a desert climate, but also because of the dramatic difference in location. Whereas Taliesin, Wisconsin, extends out over a lush, verdant valley from the brow of a hill, Taliesin West rises from a flat mesa beneath the shadow of the McDowell Mountains. Taliesin has long periods of freezing weather in winter, while there is little or no frost at Taliesin West.

In designing exterior spaces, Wright realized that he wanted extensive outdoor rooms for large gatherings. Sunset in particular was a favourite time for him to sit outdoors, converse with his family and students, and watch dramatic red, orange and yellow colours streak across the horizon. The most important outdoor room at Taliesin is the Sunset Patio. This has a textured concrete floor, sculpture around the perimeter, walls for shelter, and views out into the wild desert. Palo verde trees shade parts of the Sunset Patio, but Wright also had portable canopies that could be erected to provide shade wherever he needed it. He also established a private area enclosed by a high wall where he could sit and sunbathe or read without interruption

Wright recognized that he and his students needed spaces for recreation. He designated areas for lawn, dipping pools to provide respite from the heat, and ball courts for playing badminton.

Wright wanted his own fruit trees. Above all he loved freshly squeezed orange juice, and so an area between the drafting room and the mountain was mostly planted with different varieties of citrus. He wanted flowering trees to denote the change of seasons, especially spring time when most desert flowers bloom, following winter rainfall. And so he used bougainvillea and orchid trees (especially

A desert garden near Taliesin West, at the Desert Botanical Garden, Phoenix, Arizona, featuring an assortment of desert wildflowers, including wild sage, wild penstemon and saguaro cactus.

" It was another Eden. "

WRIGHT EXPLAINING THE APPEAL OF THE DESERT
WILDERNESS HE ACQUIRED TO BUILD TALIESIN WEST

Saguaro cactus in moonlight among palo verde trees.

Bauhinia variegata). But most of all Wright wanted to be surrounded by the most dominant of desert plants for their sculptural beauty and pattern. Palo verde trees not only resemble weeping willows, they bloom with clouds of yellow flowers in spring; ocotillo (*Fouquieria splendens*) displays flaming red tubular flower clusters in spring, atop long, wand-like prickly stalks. He liked the evergreen creosote bush for its blizzard of yellow star-shaped flowers in spring and its network of brittle branches, and above all the majestic saguaro cactus (*Carnegiea gigantea*) that can tower to heights of 60 feet with side branches that resemble columns. For Wright it produced the most satisfying skyline silhouette.

Wright not only planted his favourite indigenous desert plants in the ground around the house, he created special raised planters, using stones from the desert, to present a tapestry of colours, forms and textures from desert plants. These arrangements feature several levels of interest tall plantings of palo verde and saguaro that extend beyond head height; medium height groupings of barrel-like fishhook cactus and teddy bear cholla; and low, spreading ground covers of ice plants and brittlebush.

The following list of attractive desert plants is based on plantings Wright established in a raised bed at Taliesin West. Over the years this bed has changed because large desert plants like saguaro cactus, ocotillo and joshua trees, are susceptible to damage from floods and high winds.

Brittle bush

cially beautiful when seen in the company of the blue arroya lupin (*Lupinus succulentus*), creating an uplifting blue and orange colour harmony. Seed of California poppy is best sown directly into its flowering position in autumn to flower in early spring, though early spring sowing will generally flower by early summer. Plants self-seed readily. They make a beautiful edging to raised planters at Taliesin West. All zones.

Claret cup cactus (*Echinocereus triglochidiatus*)

The desert surrounding Taliesin West is filled with flowering cacti, especially at Pinnacle Peak, a short distance north, where Wright liked to hike and picnic with his wife. None is more beautiful in bloom than the claret cup, with its scarlet flowers and golden yellow cluster of stamens. Plants grow thick cylindrical stems up to 4ft/1.2m high, with sharp spines arranged in a star pattern. Propagation is from seed or by removing segments from the main stem and planting into moist gravel. Zones 8–11.

Century plant (*Agave* species)

Though mostly native to the deserts of Mexico, many century plant species thrive at Taliesin West, including *A. americana* 'Marginata' – the variegated century plant. Plants produce a cluster of upright, broad, spiny leaves up to 6ft/1.8m high. From the middle, after at least ten years of growth, a tall flower spike emerges, up to 20ft/6m tall, and topped with an immense cluster of greeny-yellow tubular flowers that are attractive to hummingbirds. The succulent leaves are blue-green with a yellow stripe down each edge. After flowering the plant dies, but the flower spike produces hundreds of offsets that drop to the ground and root around the mother plant. The variegated century plant looks especially attractive planted in a container. Zones 8–11.

Chain-fruit cholla (*Cylindropuntia fulgida*)

Resembling a giant teddy bear cactus, this tree-like cactus native to the Sonoran Desert grows a main trunk with cantilevered thick side branches topped by clusters of oblong spiny segments, presenting a dramatic silhouette.

California poppy

Claret cup cactus

Century plant

Brittle bush (*Encelia farinosa*)

This short-lived evergreen shrub is native to the southwestern United States and lights up the desert in spring with masses of yellow daisy-like flowers that resemble signet marigolds. Plants grow to 4ft/1.2m high, form a mound of blue-green triangular leaves and brittle stems which exude an aromatic gum when cut. Best sheared after flowering to maintain a compact, tidy appearance. Zones 8–11.

California poppy (*Eschscholzia californica*)

This prolific flowering annual flaunts its shimmering orange petals across vast stretches of the Sonoran desert, sometimes in drifts that can cover several acres. It is espe-

This desert garden features the contrasting textures of golden barrel cactus, chain cholla, yucca and creosote bush – the last is so called because it smells of creosote after rain.

Although it starts to grow upright, it quickly becomes top heavy and will arch its branches to the ground, allowing plants to cascade over terraces and rock ledges. A plant at Taliesin West, with masses of upright branches up to 12ft/3.6m tall, and also cascading branches, eventually had to be removed as it partially blocked a pathway where visitors kept walking into the spiny segments. Pink flowers in late spring produce green fruits. Zones 9–11.

Fishhook barrel cactus (*Ferocactus* species).

At least 25 of these plump species are sold in nurseries. These are mostly green with white spines, but *F. acanthoides* stands out conspicuously in desert plantings on account of its red hooked spines. Mature specimens can grow to create a 6ft/1.8m column. Flowers appear in spring or summer, depending on species. They cluster around the crown in mostly yellow, but also orange and red, followed by yellow fruits. 9 11.

Joshua tree (*Yucca brevifolia*).

Native to the Sonoran Desert, and especially prolific at Joshua Tree National Park, near Palm Springs, California, the Joshua tree features a spiny trunk with thick, snaking limbs that are topped by explosions of sharp, pointed green

evergreen leaves. White, arching flower clusters appear from the centre of each leaf cluster in spring. Plants grow to 40ft/12m high, and create a dramatic silhouette against desert sunrises and sunsets. Zones 9–10.

Jojoba (*Simmondsia chinensis*)

Also native to the Sonoran Desert, these bushy evergreen plants have small, oval, grey-green leaves and small yellow flowers that appear in spring. These produce oval, acorn-shaped brown nuts with an oil content as pure as whale oil, and useful in cosmetics and as an industrial lubricant. Plants grow to 6ft/1.8m, but can be kept low by pruning to form a dense knit of branches and a decorative hedge. Zones 9–12.

Fishhook cactus

Mesquite (*Prosopis* species)

Several species of mesquite are native the southern United States, but the two most commonly seen at Taliesin West are the honey mesquite (*P. glandulosa*, a native of Texas) and velvet mesquite (*P. velutina*, a native of Arizona). Of similar appearance, both are deciduous small trees with slender leaflets that produce a soft, feathery appearance. The snaking trunks and tortuous branches have rough dark brown bark that produces a dramatic sculptural silhouette. Mesquite is popular as a firewood, especially to barbecue meats since the wood burns hot and imparts a robust flavour. The yellow catkin-like flowers appear in spring, followed by yellow curling seedpods. Plants are especially beautiful in raised planters and pruned of their lower branches to accentuate the textured, twisting main trunk and scaffold branches. Zones 7–11.

Palo verde (*Cercidium* species)

The common name in Spanish means green tree and refers to two species with greenish bark native to the south-western United States. The blue palo verde (*C. floridum*) is the first to bloom, creating a billowing cloud of yellow flowers in spring and then 2–3in/5–7cm seed pods. A wide-spreading tree with a rounded crown, plants grow to 25ft/7.6m and equally wide. Bark and branches are blue-green, covered in small blue-green leaves. The little leaf palo verde (*C. micro-*

Joshua tree

Jojoba

Saguaro cactus (LEFT) and Palo verde (RIGHT)

Sand verbena
OPPOSITE: Mesquite

phyllum) is similar in appearance to the blue, but the bark and leaves and bright green. The flowers are a paler yellow and the brown seed pods slightly larger. Zones 9–11.

Saguaro cactus (*Carnegiea gigantea*)

No plant identifies the Sonoran Desert more than the giant saguaro cactus. Prolific on both the US and Mexican side of the border, its greatest natural concentration is south of Tucson where the Saguaro National Park protects a forest of plants. In its mature form it is unmistakable, forming a main central, fluted green column up to 60ft/18m tall, and side columns that resemble upturned arms. Up to fifteen side columns can occur on a single plant. Sanguaros grow slowly and are long lived, up to 250 years. In early summer the tip of each column will grow a crown of cup-shaped white flowers pollinated mostly by bats. Wright liked to look out from his Sunset Patio at Taliesin West and see giant saguaro silhouetted against a desert sunset, so much so that he moved huge plants from the neighbouring slopes to form sculptural accents within his view. Zones 9–11.

Sand verbena (*Abronia villosa*)

This low-growing flowering annual is native to the Sonoran Desert and self-seeds readily to create mounded mats of blue-green foliage just 12in/30cm high and up to 3ft/90cm wide, covered in spring with clusters of bright pink flowers. Useful as an edging to beds and borders, also spilling over the edge of a container. Zones 8–10.

Spanish bayonet (*Yucca aloifolia*)

Native to the southern United States, the Spanish bayonet is one of the most ornamental of desert yucca, since it develops a strong trunk, topped by radiating bayonet-shaped evergreen, spiny leaves. Plants grow to 10ft/3m high and produce a candelabra of conspicuous white flowers in spring. Two massed plantings of Spanish bayonet occupy parallel beds in the forecourt at Taliesin West, creating what appears to be a clump of palms. Zones 8–11. Other species of yucca, such as *Y. filamentosa*, are hardy to zone 5.

Spanish bayonet

Teddy bear cholla

OPPOSITE: Picturesque desert plants near Taliesin in the Sonoran Desert, showing teddy bear cholla, fishhook barrel cactus, and both yellow and white forms of brittle bush.

Teddy bear cholla (*Cylindropuntia bigelovii*)

The teddy bear cholla usually grows a single straight trunk topped by clusters of yellow sausage-shaped spiny segments that glow when backlit. From a distance they appear to be soft and fuzzy but in fact can inflict painful injury if touched. At Taliesin West, colonies of teddy bear cholla are conspicuous beyond the boundary walls in the desert wilderness. Plants grow to 8ft/2.4m high, and though not long lived, each segment can detach easily from the mother plant and root in gravelly soil. Green flowers occur in spring, followed by yellow fruits. Zones 9–11.

Flowers that attract hummingbirds

A large number of desert wildflowers attract hummingbirds for pollination. The flowers are mostly spire-like and tube-shaped, in shades of red – the most attractive colour for hummingbirds. Some of the showiest include species of agave (see above) agastache, penstemon and salvia, such as *Agastache rupestris*, *Penstemon parryi* and *Salvia coccinea*.

***

Originally, Wright wanted only native desert plants at Taliesin West, but after a number of people complained about injuries from the sharp spines of cactus and some of the desert shrubs, he relegated the worst offenders beyond the footprint of the property, allowing some dry climate plants, mostly from Africa and South America, to replace them. In particular, he introduced the yellow Lady Banks' rose (*Rosa banksiae*) from China, Italian cypress from the Mediterranean, bougainvillea and orchid trees (*Bauhinia purpurea*) from Brazil, and the Indian rubber tree (*Ficus elastica*), in addition to a number of colourful dry-climate flowering annuals – mainly from African deserts – such as calendula, African daisies, and gazanias.

Ten landscape tips from FRANK LLOYD WRIGHT

The following nuggets of advice are gleaned from many sources – mostly his autobiography, lectures, magazine articles and comments he made to staff and students.

- Expose the house foundation to show where it meets the ground. Although he once quipped, "Doctors can bury their mistakes. Architects can plant vines," Wright particularly disliked shrubbery hiding his artistry. For example, he admired Japanese maples but he liked to plant them in other parts of the garden, not around the house foundation. To soften hard architectural lines he preferred to plant trailing vines in dish planters on pedestals and window box planters. This draping effect then helped the building blend with nature.

- Where an exposed site needs plantings for shelter or aesthetic appeal, first consider the use of indigenous plants as these are likely to be more reliable and require less maintenance than non-natives. At Taliesin Wright planted native bur oaks as lone tree accents, weeping willows around his lake and sumac for brilliant autumn colour and tortuous trunks. However, he firmly believed that a tree inappropriately placed (such as blocking a scenic view), should be considered a weed and taken out.

- Flower colour among plants is secondary to texture, shape and form. However, Wright did like to have flowering trees and shrubs for fleeting colour, and also perennials as they come back every year, and can provide armloads of flowers for cutting to create indoor floral arrangements.

- Try to make your home landscape distinctive. When Wright began gardening at Taliesin West in the Sonoran Desert, the local practice was to eliminate desert plants such as cacti in favour of non-native "exotics", not only owing to the over-familiarity of the natives, but also their spiny nature. Wright, however, saw the use of desert natives as vital in making his winter home part of the desert and to create interesting sculptural accents.

- Allow trees and shrubs to grow naturally. Learn the art of pruning by purchasing a good book. Trees and shrubs that outgrow their boundaries can be carefully sized back and still look natural. Do not trim shrubs into topiary shapes so severely that they look like meat balls.

- Take as much interest in the house surroundings as you do the house interior. Plant for privacy and shelter as well as aesthetic appeal.

- Create vistas where none exist and preserve vistas that have become obscured by vegetation. A view of water – a lake or river – is especially desirable.

- Consider a vine-covered pergola leading from the house to a garden room or between two sunny garden spaces. This produces a leafy tunnel and a sense of compression, then release, when you emerge into the sunlight.

- Use sculpture as focal points, particularly at the end of a path or entrance to a garden space. But choose sculpture in scale with its surroundings.

- Digest other garden styles such as French formality, Italian baroque and Japanese imperial, but do not slavishly copy them. Monet, for example, was inspired by Japanese art to create his water garden. A Japanese-style arched bridge, weeping willows edging the pond and water lilies on its surface, give it a Japanese aura, but it is devoid of other stylized Japanese elements such as stone lanterns, bonsai'd trees, stepping stones and a tea house that would have been jarring in his corner of the Normandy countryside.

VISITING WRIGHT'S LANDSCAPES and other sites

Information about visiting Wright's gardens and other related locations is given below. Phone numbers specified are from within the US. Use the prefix 001 when calling from outside the US.

WRIGHT'S LANDSCAPES

Wright's name is world famous as an architect. His gardens at Taliesin and Taliesin West justify Cornelia Brierly's claim that he was the greatest landscape architect who ever lived. Moreover, his Fallingwater design is undoubtedly the most recognizable house in the world, largely because Wright had the nerve to place it above a scenic waterfall instead of facing it. He respected the natural qualities of a site and enhanced the impression of naturalness and timeless qualities of a property by knowing what to preserve and what to add. The best way to appreciate Wright's genius for landscaping is to start by visiting the four properties that are the focus of this book. If possible, go in chronological order, first to his home and studio at Oak Park, Illinois; then his summer home Taliesin, Wisconsin; next his winter home Taliesin West, Scottsdale Arizona; and save until last, Fallingwater, in the Laurel Highlands of Pennsylvania.

OAK PARK

At Oak Park, lilacs Wright planted still bloom in spring, but most impressive are certain structural accents – his *Boulder* statues, the dish planters he designed, the *wise bird* sculptures. Dominating the back courtyard is a champion-size ginkgo tree, offering cool shade in summer and a blizzard of golden leaves in autumn. The house interior has been restored to the time of Wright's last year of occupancy, minus his palm collection, but with examples of his glasswork, murals, and dried plant arrangements intact. For further information call (708) 848-1978 or go to the website www.wrightplus.org.

After visiting the Oak Park house you can explore the neighbourhood streets that feature Wright-designed houses; you can take a self-guided tour using a map provided by the gift shop at Wright's home. (At the end of Forest Avenue be sure to visit Austin Park, with a bust and fence design commemorating Wright's work.) It is then an easy four-hour drive by Interstate highway to Spring Green, Wisconsin, for a tour of Taliesin.

TALIESIN

In partnership with Taliesin's owner, the Frank Lloyd Wright Foundation, the private non-profit Taliesin Preservation Inc, works to preserve Wright's Wisconsin property, its gardens and six major buildings. Guided tours of the site are conducted from the Visitor's Center from May to October. For tour information call (608) 588-7900, or visit www.TaliesinPreservation.org.

A choice of tours is available to visitors but, before you take the tour, drive along Rt. 23 and park at the stone pillars marking the original entrance. From here you can take in a complete panoramic view of the property – Taliesin residence in the brow of the hill to the right, Midway Farm with its sleek red barn extending out from a wooded ridge to the left, and behind it the Romeo and Juliet windmill; then further left the red gables of Hillside Home School where apprentices in the Taliesin Fellowship live and work in a drafting room that represents Wright's abstraction of a pine forest.

Return to the Visitor's Center, which Wright designed as a restaurant and which still serves meals, to take a guided tour. The bridge to Spring Green, crossing the Wisconsin River, is within walking distance, allowing a view of the river, its sandbars and the wooded hilltop where Wright's house is located.

I stayed overnight at the House on the Rock Resort, a half mile from the visitor's centre. Designed by a graduate of the Wright Fellowship, the hotel has spectacular views over land previously owned by Wright. It now features a spectacular golf course.

WRIGHT'S GRAVESITE

Wright enjoyed a long and distinguished career, but also he suffered periods of financial hardship and personal tragedy few could survive. Above all, a visit to Wright's gravesite in the grounds of Unity Chapel, within sight of Taliesin, should not be missed, for there is the grave of Mamah Cheney whose love inspired Wright to build Taliesin and

then rebuild it following her untimely death and its destruction by fire, and produce what architectural critic Robert Campbell has described as "the greatest single building in America."

TALIESIN WEST

Taliesin West can be visited at any time of year, but the first week of April – when the desert starts to bloom – is best. Guided tours will take you through the living quarters and out onto the terraces. The contrast between Taliesin – in a temperate climate and Taliesin West, in a sub-tropical desert climate, is amazing. For tour and other information, call (480) 860-2700 or visit www.franklloydwright.org. I stayed at the nearby Four Seasons Hotel, Troon, and from the hotel enjoyed walks to one of Wright's favourite picnic spots, Pinnacle Peak State Park.

FALLINGWATER

Fallingwater is a thirty-minute drive south of the Pennsylvania Turnpike, at Mill Run, on route 381. Again, admission to the house is only through guided tours. Tours gather in the visitor's centre then take a short walk to the bridge spanning Bear Run, and the entrance to the main residence. Visitors also walk uphill to the guest house, and then are free to walk nature trails for views at all angles. Although the property is beautiful in all seasons, I like spring the best, when the leaves are newly unfurled and the dogwoods bloom, but also autumn is spectacular when the maples turn colour. No matter what the season, in rain or shine, it is an experience you will never forget.

Remarkably, for his architectural services at Fallingwater Wright charged a modest $8,000, plus an additional $4,500.00 for items of furniture he designed. The home, together with guest and servants' quarters cost a total of $150,000 to build when Pennsylvania's minimum wage was 25 cents an hour.

Fallingwater is open all year (weekends only during winter months). Entry to the house costs $15.00, and entry to the grounds, with more than a thousand acres of woodland trails, is $6.00. For more information call 724-329-8501 or visit www.wpconserve.org.

KENTUCK KNOB

Seven miles from Fallingwater, located on Kentuck Road, between Chalk Hill and Mill Run, Pennsylvania, Kentuck Knob is open year round. "Although we are not as as well known as Fallingwater, we are fortunate to be close enough to draw many visitors from there," says Director Cathy Ciaccia. The property enjoys 30,000 visitors a year, their entrance fees allowing the property to be self-sufficient, covering general overhead, plus maintenance and administration staff of seven people. For further information call 724-329-1901 or visit www.kentuckknob.com.

Cathy Ciaccia explained that a big problem is maintaining the labyrinth of woodland trails, by judicious pruning of aggressive undergrowth and clean-up of fallen branches after storms. Its original owner, Mrs Bernadine Hagan, planted thousands of native trees, but unfortunately most of the dogwoods have died, leaving gaps. Mrs Hagan initially tried to create a Japanese-style moss garden around the house but this was unsuccessful because of the high elevation. Then woodland wildflowers were tried, such as foam flowers, trillium, jonquils, bleeding heart, wild blue phlox, native wild ginger and dwarf cyclamen, and these flourished. "For $3,000.00 plus the cost of moving it, we also acquired a greenhouse purchased from Fallingwater, which I used to house my bonsai collection and bromeliads," wrote Mrs. Hagan who is now 95 and resident in nearby Unionville. The greenhouse today serves as a café, attached to the visitor's centre.

Mrs. Hagan would move her bonsai collection to a flagstone patio and Japanese-style rock garden at the rear of the house during frost-free months, enhancing the Japanese feel, and so new plantings of Japanese maple have been made to replace trees that suffered damage from harsh winters, and still evoke the appearance of a Japanese woodland garden.

When Peter, Lord Palumbo, purchased Kentuck Knob from Mrs. Hagen in 1986, he wrote at settlement: "Very few people have the vision and the foresight to commission great works of art, but you belong indelibly to that small and distinguished band. As the beneficiary of this far-sightedness, I am grateful indeed, and want to assure you that I shall respect the property," – which he has done in exemplary style, allowing visitors to view the grounds, his collection of modern sculpture, and also the house interior which is furnished but unoccupied. Lord Palumbo explains: "Though we live in England most of the year, my family and I visit Kentuck Knob for long intervals, but rather than live in the house and interfere with tours, we prefer to stay in a nearby farmhouse."

NEMACOLIN, PENNSYLVANIA

Both Fallingwater and Kentuck Knob can be seen in a day, but visitors are encouraged to stay at least one night at a nearby property that has accommodation influenced by Wright's design for the Imperial Hotel, in Tokyo, which unfortunately was largely demolished in the 1960's in order to add more rooms. Called Nemacolin Woodlands and named for an Indian chief who supported General George Washington during the American Revolution, the property offers two main hotel facilities. They are the Chateau, which is a full-scale replica of the fabulous Ritz Hotel in Paris, and Falling Rock, which is inspired by Wright's design for the Imperial Hotel, Tokyo. Set in almost 3,000 acres of woodland and rolling hills, the property is owned by the founder of the 84 Lumber Company, Joseph A. Hardy III. It includes 36 holes of golf, stables, rock climbing facilities, clay pigeon shooting, a spa and miles of nature trails. The grounds of the Chateau and Falling Rock are beautifully landscaped with perennial gardens, a water feature that resembles designs by Jens Jensen, art galleries and garden sculpture. Call 866-554-6957 for more information or visit www.nemacolin.com .

JENS JENSEN'S "THE CLEARING"

Wright shared ideals with and was influenced by his friend the Danish-born landscape designer Jens Jensen, and lectured at "The Clearing", the school Jensen established on a high promontory overlooking the waters of Green Bay, Wisconsin. Today The Clearing educates and informs the public about the legacy of Jens Jensen. Influenced by the folk schools of his native Denmark, it offers a wide range of classes, including painting, writing,

quilting, birding, wood carving, music, weaving, philosophy, stained glass, metal work, nature study, and gardening.

For more information about The Clearing's work, and especially its summer program, which runs from May to October, visit www.theclearing. org. The Clearing's mission today is "To provide diverse educational experiences in the folk school tradition, in a setting of quiet forests, meadows and water. The Clearing is a place where adults who share an interest in nature, arts and the humanities can learn, reflect and wonder ."

WRIGHT'S SITES OPEN FOR PUBLIC TOURS

The following sites are open to the public. Times and dates are constantly changing so call ahead to confirm current status.

A.D. German Warehouse 300 South Church Street, Richland Center, Wisconsin 53581. (608) 647-2808 or (800) 422-1318.

Allen-Lambe House 255 North Roosevelt Street, Wichita, Kansas 67208. (316) 687-1027.

Annunciation Greek Orthodox Church 9400 West Congress, Milwaukee, Wisconsin 53225. (414) 461-9400.

Arizona Biltmore Resort Missouri and 24th Street, Phoenix, Arizona 85016. (602) 955-6600.

Beth Sholom Synagogue 8231 Old York Road, Elkins Park, Pennsylvania 19027. (215) 887-1342.

Blue Sky Mausoleum Forest Lawn Cemetery, 1411 Delaware Avenue, Buffalo, New York 14209. (716) 885-1600.

Buffalo's Rowing Boathouse 194 Porter Avenue, Buffalo, New York (716) 362-3140.

Cedar Rock Quasquerton, Iowa 52326. (319) 934-3140. April-November.

Charnley-Perskey House 1365 North Astor Street, Chicago, Illinois 60610. (312) 915-0105.

Community Christian Church 4601 Main Street, Kansas City, Missouri 64112. (816) 561-6531.

Dana-Thomas House 301 East Lawrence Avenue, Springfield, Illinois 62703. (217) 782-6776.

Duncan House Donegal, Pennsylvania. This house was moved from Lisle, Illinois to the Laurel Highlands of Pennsylvania, close to Fallingwater. It is a prefabricated Usonian, one of nine of its type ever built, reconstructed on the 120-acre Polymath Park estate. Tours and overnight accommodation are available. (800) 458-4680.

Fabayan Villa 1511 South Batavia Avenue, Geneva, Illinois 60134. (630) 232-4811.

Fallingwater PO Box R, Mill Run, Pennsylvania 15464. (714) 329-8501. Mid-March-November.

Florida Southern College 111 Hollingsworth Drive, Lakeland, Florida 33801. (863) 680-4110.

Frances Little House II Living room reconstruction, Metropolitan Museum of Art, New York, NY 10028. (212) 535-7710. Library reconstruction, the Allentown Art Museum, Allentown, PA 18101. (610) 432-4333

Gordon House The Oregon Garden, 879 West Main Street, Silverton, OR 97381. (877) 674-2733.

Grady Gammage Memorial Auditorium Arizona State University Campus, Gammage Parkway and Apache Blvd, Tempe, AZ 85287. (480) 965-4050.

Graycliff 6472 Lake Shore Road, Derby, NY 14047. (716) 947-9217.

Guggenheim Museum (Solomon R. Guggenheim Museum) 1071 Fifth Avenue, New York, NY 10128. (212) 423-3774

Hanna House Stanford University, Stanford, CA 94305. (650) 725-8352.

John J. Haynes House Usonian house available for overnight rentals, Fort Wayne, IN. Visit

Hollyhock House 4800 Hollywood Blvd, Los Angeles, CA 90027. (323) 644-66269.

Imperial Hotel Lobby Reconstructed at the Museum Meiji-mura, 1 Uchiyama, Inuyamashi, Aichi Prefecture, 484-0000, Japan. (0568) 67-0314.

Jiyu Gakuen Myonichikan This Wright-designed school building includes a museum of Wright's Japanese projects. 2-31-3 Nishiikebukuro Toshima-ku, Tokyo, Japan. 81-3-3971-7535

Johnson Administration Building 1525 Howe Street, Racine, WI 53403. (262) 260-2154

Kalita Humphreys Theater Dallas Theater Center, 3636 Turtle Creek Blvd, Dallas, TX 75219. (214) 252-3921.

Kentuck Knob P. O. Box 305, Chalk Hill, PA 15421. (724) 329-1901.

Kraus House 120 N. Ballas Rd., St. Louis, MO 63122. (314) 822-8359.

Marin County Civic Center 3501 Civic Center Dr., San Rafael, CA 94903. (415) 499-3237.

Martin House Complex 125 Jewett Parkway, Buffalo, NY 14214. (716) 856-3858.

Meyer May House 450 Madison Ave. SE, Grand Rapids, MI 49503. (616) 246-4821.

Monona Terrace Community & Convention Center One John Nolen Dr., Madison, WI 53703. (608) 261-4015.

Nakoma Clubhouse County Rd. A-15, Clio, CA (50

miles north of Lake Tahoe via Hwy 89N). (877) 418-0880.

Oak Park Home & Studio Guided tours Mon.-Fri., 11 am, 1 pm & 3 pm, every 45 minutes. Sat. & Sun., 11 am-330 pm, every 20 minutes. Self-guided audio walking tours also available. Oak Park Historic District, daily 10 am-330 pm. Guided exterior tours at 11 am, then every hour from 11 am –4 pm weekends only. Ginkgo Tree Bookshop, 951 Chicago Ave., Oak Park, IL 60302. (708) 848-1978. www.wrightplus.org.

Seth Peterson Cottage E9982 Fern Dell Rd., Lake Delton, WI 53940. (608) 254-6551.

Pettit Chapel Belvidere Cemetery Office, 1121 N. Main St., Belvidere, IL 61008. (815) 547-7642.

Pope-Leighey House 9000 Richmond Hwy., Alexandria, VA 22309. (703) 780-4000.

Price Tower 6th St. & Dewey Ave., Bartlesville, OK 74003. (918) 336-4949.

Robie House 5757 S. Woodlawn Ave., Chicago, IL 60637. (773) 834-1847.

Rosenbaum House 601 Riverview Dr., Florence, AL 35630. (256) 740-8899.

Stockman House 530 First St. NE, Mason City, IA 50401. (641) 423-1923.

Taliesin & Hillside Open for tours May 1-Oct. 31. Hillside Studio & Theater Tour, daily 1030 am – 430 pm. Taliesin House Tour (daily 10 am – 3 pm). No children under 12. Taliesin Estate Tour, 930 am, reservations required. Highlights Tour (daily 1045 am & 215 pm) 2-hours. Taliesin Sunset Tour (June-August, Fridays only at 5 pm. reservations required. No children under 12 allowed on Estate, Highlights or Sunset tours. Tours begin at the Frank Lloyd Wright Visitor Center, located at the intersection of Highways 23 & C, across from the Taliesin estate. For information or tour reservations, call (877) 588-7900. P. O. Box 399, Spring Green, WI 53588. www.taliesinpreservation.org.

Taliesin West Guided tours. WINTER HOURS, Nov.-April 1-hour PANORAMA, daily 915am-415pm, tours offered every half hour; 90-minute INSIGHTS, daily 9am-4pm, tours offered every half hour; 3-hour BEHIND THE SCENES, Mon. Thurs. & Sat., 9am. (Reservations suggested, but not required); 2-hour DESERT

WALK, daily 10am & 3pm; 2 hour APPRENTICE 'SHELTER' TOUR, Dec. 2-April 14, Sat., 115 pm. 2-hour Night Lights on THE DESERT TOUR Feb. (Fri. nights only), March-Aug. (Thurs. & Fri.) 6, 630 & 7pm. (Reservations suggested, but not required); SUMMER HOURS, May 1-Oct. 31 No tours Tues. & Wed. in July-August. 90 minute PANORAMA + SHELTER, 9, 10 & 11 am.; 90-minute SUMMER INSIGHTS, daily 930 & 1130 am and 12, 1, 2, 3 & 4 pm. (also offered 1030 am May, Sept. & Oct.); 3-hour BEHIND THE SCENES, Mon. & Sat., 9 am. (also offered Thursdays at 9 am May, Sept. & Oct.) (Reservations suggested, but not required); 90-minute CREATIVE ARCHITECTURE TOUR, daily, 1030 am & 130 pm (June-August). Group tours available. Cactus Rd. & Frank Lloyd Wright Blvd., Scottsdale, AZ 85261. (480) 860-2700. For a pre-recorded message (480) 860-8810. www.franklloydwright.org.

Unitarian Meeting House 900 University Bay Dr., Madison, WI 53705. (608) 233-9774, ext. 10.

Unity Temple 875 Lake St., Oak Park, IL 60301. (708) 383-8873.

Weltzheimer Johnson House, Oberlin, OH. For directions (440) 775-8665.

Westcott House 1340 East High Street, Springfield, OH 45503. (937) 327-9291.

Wingspread 33 East Four Mile Rd., Racine, WI 53402. (262) 681-3353.

Zimmerman House 201 Myrtle Way, Manchester, NH 03104. (603) 669-6144 ext. 108.

CHRONOLOGY

1856 Lloyd Jones family arrives from Wales and settles in the Wisconsin River valley to farm.

1867 Birth of Frank Lloyd Wright, June 8, in Richland Center, Wisconsin.

1879 After moving from one parish to another, Wright's family moves to Madison, Wisconsin. Frank spends summers on an uncle's farm near Spring Green.

1884 Wright's parents divorce and Frank has no further contact with his father.

1886 Wright attends the University of Wisconsin and takes courses in civil engineering.

1887 Wright moves to Chicago to work for Joseph Lyman Silsbee, as a tracer – copying architectural plans when duplicates are needed.

1888 Wright starts work for leading Chicago architects, Adler & Sullivan.

1890 Wright marries Catherine Lee Tobin and they build a home on property purchased from a nurseryman by Wright's mother. Wright's first of six children, Frank Lloyd Wright Jr. is born the same year.

1892 Wright is dismissed from Adler & Sullivan when Sullivan recognizes a house as Wright's design and considers his moonlighting as a breach of their agreement

1898 Wright adds a studio to his home.

1900 Wright designs his first prairie-style house, a blending of Japanese architecture and prairie patterns, and he is kept busy with commissions, mostly for residences in the Oak Park area.

1905 Wright leaves for Japan with his wife Catherine, staying six months.

1909 Wright leaves his family and moves to Europe with Mamah Borthwick Cheney. He works with a German publisher on a portfolio of his architectural designs.

1911 Wright begins work on a new home for himself and Mrs Cheney, at Taliesin, near Spring Green, Wisconsin.

1914 Mrs Cheney and her two young children, plus four of Wright's staff, are murdered when a servant embarks on a mad rampage. The house burns to the ground.

1915 Wright begins a relationship with Miriam Noel, a sculptress, and she moves to Taliesin, marrying her after his divorce becomes final, in 1923.

1916–22 Wright spends long periods in Japan, working on the Imperial Hotel, Tokyo.

1923 Wright's mother, Anna dies. He does not attend her funeral, following bitter disagreements over the suitability of Miriam as a wife.

1923–35 Wright establishes an office in California where he sees great potential for a new style of architecture inspired by Mayan architecture. He completes five notable commissions using textured cement blocks, supervised by his eldest son.

1925 Wright meets Olgivanna (Olga) Ivanova Hinzenberg at the opera, a married woman with a child. Their own daughter, Iovanna is born the same year and Olgivanna moves to Taliesin. A second fire, started during a thunderstorm, destroys Taliesin for the second time.

1927 Wright divorces Miriam, blaming her cocaine addiction for their break-up. He sells shares in his enterprise to stave off bankruptcy due to the recession and lack of commissions. He begins an autobiography.

1928 Wright and Olgivanna are married. She is thirty years his junior.

1929 Wright establishes a camp near Phoenix, Arizona, and purchases property for the establishment of Taliesin West as a winter home and teaching facility.

1932 Wright and Olgivanna establish the Taliesin Fellowship to teach architecture.

1935–36 Wright's career picks up. He designs Fallingwater and the Johnson Wax headquarters. The first Usonian house is built – his answer to affordable, distinctive homes. These mostly feature a spacious living area, but small kitchen and bathroom; also no basement or attic.

1937 Fallingwater completed and media coverage of the event is so favourable it makes Wright a celebrity.

1943–1959 Wright designs and is involved with the building of the Guggenheim Museum, New York.

1959 Wright dies at Taliesin West aged ninety-one, and six months before the completion of the Guggenheim Museum. He is originally buried in the graveyard of Unity Church, within sight of Taliesin, and close to the gravesite of Mrs. Cheney. (When Olgivanna died in 1985, his remains were moved to Taliesin West to be buried with Olgivanna).

BIBLIOGRAPHY

A vast amount of material was written by Frank Lloyd Wright about his design sensitivity, and since his death publi shers have released numerous publications covering all aspects of his life. During my research and analysis of Wright's landscaping philosophy, I found the following publications invaluable.

Death in a Prairie House: Frank Lloyd Wright and the Taliesin Murders by William R. Drennan (University of Wisconsin Press, 2007).

Desert Life by Cornelia Brierly (Frank Lloyd Wright Foundation, 1988).

Fallingwater: Frank Lloyd Wright's Romance with Nature by Lynda S. Waggoner (Universe, 1996).

Frank Lloyd Wright: An Autobiography by Frank Lloyd Wright (Duell, Sloan and Pearce, 1943).

Frank Lloyd Wright and Taliesin by Frances Nemtin (Pomegranate Communications, 2000).

Frank Lloyd Wright: Designs for an American Landscape 1922-1932 ed. David G. De Long (Harry N. Abrams, 1996).

Frank Lloyd Wright's Fallingwater by Ezra Stoller (Princeton Architectural Press, 1999).

Frank Lloyd Wright, Taliesin West by Bruce Brooks Pfeiffer (ADA Edita, 1980).

Frank Lloyd Wright, The Lost Years, 1910-1922 by Anthony Alofsen (University of Chicago Press, 1994).

Frank Lloyd Wright: The Mike Wallace Interviews by Mike Wallace (VHS and DVD containing two 1957 television interviews).

Jens Jensen: Maker of Natural Parks and Gardens by Robert E. Grese (Johns Hopkins University Press, 1992).

1001 Gardens You Must See Before You Die ed. Rae Spencer-Jones (Barrons, 2007).

Siftings by Jens Jensen (Johns Hopkins University Press, reprinted 1990).

Tales of Taliesin by Cornelia Brierly (Pomegranate Communications, 2000).

Web of Life by Frances Nemtin (self published 2001).

Windows of Taliesin by Frances Nemtin (Kramer Printing, 2006).

Wrightscapes: Frank Lloyd Wright's Landscape Designs by Charles E. and Berdeana Aguar (McGraw-Hill, 2002).